Conservation
Finance Handbook

THE TRUST FOR PUBLIC LAND'S

CONSERVATION
FINANCE HANDBOOK

HOW COMMUNITIES ARE PAYING
FOR PARKS AND LAND CONSERVATION

KIM HOPPER
ERNEST COOK

THE TRUST FOR PUBLIC LAND
SAN FRANCISCO, CALIFORNIA

This publication is designed to provide accurate, authoritative information in regard to the subject matter covered. It is sold with the
understanding that the publisher is not engaged in rendering legal,
accounting, or other professional service. If legal advice or other
expert assistance is required, the services
of competent professionals should be sought.

Conservation finance handbook: how communities are paying for
parks and land conservation / The Trust for Public Land.
p. cm.
Includes bibliographical references and index.

Cover and text design by Y YES/O Design
Composition by Y YES/O Design

Manufactured in the United States of America.

Printed with soy inks on recycled paper by
Queen City Printers, Inc.

Published by the Trust for Public Land
116 New Montgomery, 4th Floor, San Francisco, CA 94105
1.415.495.4014

Distributed by Chelsea Green Publishing Company
85 North Main Street, White River Junction, VT 05001
1.800.639.4099

ISBN 0-9672806-4-8

10 9 8 7 6 5 4 3 2 1

Contents

Acknowledgments   VII

Introduction   IX

CHAPTER ONE   Understanding Greenprinting   1
> Exploring Federal, State, and Private Conservation
> Funding Sources   6
> Securing Local Conservation Funds: Trends and Techniques   15

CHAPTER TWO   Doing Your Homework   21
> Researching Basic Demographics and Landuse   23
> Investigating Financing Options   25
> Crunching the Numbers   26
> Researching Legal Constraints   34
> Analyzing Election Data   37

CHAPTER THREE   Measuring Public Opinion   41
> Interviewing Community Leaders   43
> Selecting a Pollster   46
> Conducting the Right Poll at the Right Time   50
> Designing and Interpreting Your Poll   51
> Considering Focus Groups   65
> Conducting a Community Assessment   69

CHAPTER FOUR   Designing a Winning Measure   73
> Defining Goals, Identifying Land, and Setting Priorities   75
> Determining the Best Time to Seek Voter Support   81
> Selecting the Funding Size and Mechanism   84
> Establishing Fiscal Safeguards   85
> Drafting Ballot Language   88

Contents (continued)

CHAPTER FIVE **Running a Conservation Campaign** 93

Keeping It Legal 94

Organizing Your Campaign 106

Designing a Winning Campaign Strategy 113

Developing a Campaign Plan and Budget 120

Raising Money 125

Securing Endorsements 136

Developing a Paid Media Plan 138

Designing Direct Mail 141

Advertising in the Newspaper 149

Producing Broadcast Media 152

Posting House Signs and Billboards 156

Working with Campaign Consultants 157

Planning for Free Media 160

Designing an Internet Campaign Strategy 166

Setting Up Your Field Organization 170

After Election Day 185

Endnotes 187

Bibliography and Resources 191

About the Trust for Public Land 196

Index 199

Acknowledgments

The handbook was written by the Trust for Public Land (TPL) consultant Kim Hopper under the direction of Ernest Cook, director of TPL's Conservation Finance Program. Helen Whybrow served as the publication's editor. TPL's Debra Summers served as the production manager.

TPL's Andy McLeod, Adam Eichberg, Will Abberger, Matt Zieper, Wendy Muzzy, Susan Ives, Debra Summers, and consultant Steven Glazer advised on the book's contents. Legal assistance was provided by TPL's Bill Lee and by Rosemary Fei, attorney at Silk, Adler & Colvin.

Thanks also to the following individuals for their assistance: Kathy Decoster (TPL), Rachel Dinno (TPL), Constance Foster (TPL), Angela Graham (TPL), Bill Johnston (The Conservation Campaign), Nicki List (TPL), Christopher Mann, Brenda Marshall (TPL), Tod McKay (Boise, Idaho, mayor's office), Lauren McLean (Boise Foothills preservation bond campaign manager), Mark Middlebrook (City of Jacksonville, Florida), William Poole (TPL), Geoff Roach (TPL), Peter Sortino (St. Louis 2004), Chris Slattery (TPL), and Cynthia Whiteford (TPL).

As contributors to TPL's *Local Open Space Financing Campaigns: A Handbook of TPL Case Studies* and other TPL publications, the following individuals provided background for this report: Corey Brown (Big Sur Land Trust and formerly with TPL), Esther Feldman (Community Conservancy International, also formerly with TPL), and Eugene Duvernoy (Cascades Land Conservancy and former TPL consultant).

Introduction

PHOTO BY JASON LANGER

Pay more to protect the land? Voters said yes to the tune of $5.7 billion in 2002, $1.7 billion in 2001, and $7.5 billion in 2000.[1] This money is now being used to protect ranchlands in Montana, wildlife habitat in Illinois, city parks in New York—and many other vital open lands.

As growth and sprawl chip away at our open space, communities are approving conservation funding measures in record numbers. These voters are coming to recognize the inter-relationship of conservation, a safe environment, a strong economy, and a livable community. And they are responding to well-designed finance measures that reflect the unique conservation needs and funding capacities of their communities.

The Trust for Public Land (TPL), a national nonprofit land conservation organization, has helped communities across the country secure billions of dollars in public and private funds for parks and open space. Through its Conservation Finance Program, TPL has championed measures of all sizes, from small grassroots campaigns at the town level to professionally managed billion-dollar campaigns at the state level—and everything in the middle. Between 1996 and 2002, TPL assisted in the passage of local and state measures that set aside more than $25 billion for parks and open space. To further expand public conservation funding, TPL created The Conservation Campaign (TCC) in May 2000. TCC is a 501(c)(4) nonpartisan lobbying affiliate that is able to lobby for government funds without limit and directly support local campaign activities.

TPL's conservation finance services are part of the organization's larger mission to help conserve land for people to enjoy as community gardens, parks, open space, and wilderness areas. TPL takes a strategic and proactive approach to conservation called "greenprinting." With greenprinting, a community plans for open space in the same way it plans for other aspects of its infrastructure—transportation and communication networks, schools, hospitals, utilities, and so on. Greenprinting is a voluntary, incentives-based, land conservation technique that is designed to steer future growth toward areas of existing development while permanently protecting networks of important land.

Greenprinting is a three-step process that includes visioning, funding, and land acquisition. This handbook is a "how-to" guide that explains step two, the complex process of securing federal, state, and private conservation funds and—most important—researching, designing, and passing a local, voter-approved conservation finance measure.

To seek voter approval for public funding, communities should first conduct thorough research and public opinion polling. This process helps proponents decide if the time is right and, if so, what size and type of measure voters are most likely to accept. Next comes the design of a measure that is fiscally prudent and publicly acceptable. There are many important components to consider, including the funding amount and type, fiscal safeguards, administering agency, and election timing, to name just a few.

Once the measure is designed, a campaign should be launched that communicates the benefits of the measure to voters. This book covers a range of campaign issues, from fundraising to field organizing to legal issues. With adequate funding in place, communities are able to implement their conservation vision, permanently protecting significant land and water resources.

We hope that this handbook finds a wide audience of public officials and staff, neighborhood leaders, community activists, land trusts, and conservationists. Knowing that the roles involved in a conservation finance effort vary, we provide tips on the entire process. If you have questions about the information in this handbook, we invite you to contact TPL's Conservation Finance Program.

We recognize that asking voters to raise their taxes or incur debt may seem daunting. Yet voter support for conservation finance measures is high across the country. I encourage you to explore the funding options in your community. With these resources, you can protect the land, water, and quality of life now and for future generations.

WILL ROGERS, PRESIDENT
THE TRUST FOR PUBLIC LAND

CHAPTER ONE

Understanding
Greenprinting

A major shift is occurring in the land conservation arena. In
the traditional model, local governments and land trusts worked
together to protect individually threatened pieces of property,
sometimes under intense development pressure. Growth was
directed but in an unplanned and fragmented way—what The Trust
for Public Land President Will Rogers refers to as "emergency
room conservation." These battles often did not serve the best
interests of communities trying to protect open space, nor deal
fairly with developers trying to respond to the demands of growth.

This reactive approach is being replaced by strategic and
comprehensive open space protection in which land conservation is used as a tool for managing growth and protecting a
community's most significant land and water resources.
Communities are getting ahead of the development curve and
putting planning front and center in the land conservation
process. Growth is accommodated where it makes sense—near
existing infrastructure—and conservation is used where it
matters most—for the farmland, waterways, wildlife habitat,
and open spaces that sustain and define a community.

The Trust for Public Land (TPL) calls this proactive approach
to conservation "greenprinting." Others may call it "green infrastructure" or "green design," but all these terms are about
protecting a community's most significant places while making
way for development that follows sensible patterns.[2]

The concept is not new: progressive urban designers and preservationists throughout the 19th and 20th centuries advocated land conservation to shape metropolitan growth and connect open spaces. A few communities, such as the city of Boulder, Colorado, have integrated land conservation and growth management for decades. What we're seeing now, however, is widespread interest in an integrated, comprehensive approach to conservation and growth management at all levels of government.[3]

What accounts for the shift? Historically, federal and state governments have worked to preserve vast landscapes and habitats, while private conservation organizations have focused on biology-based missions. In contrast, local governments must respond to local conservation challenges, priorities, and funding constraints. As growth and development transform the landscape at ever-increasing rates, local governments are seeking new techniques to

PHOTO BY ED RUSSELL

THESE MEMBERS OF FRIENDS OF HIGH ELK ARE PART OF A BROAD-BASED COALITION TO PROTECT LAND IN AND AROUND GUNNISON, COLORADO. THIS GROUP USED MAPS TO TARGET PROTECTION AREAS AND DESIGN A CONSER-VATION VISION.

THE VALUE OF OPEN SPACE

An investment in open space can yield significant returns. Consider these potential benefits:

FISCAL BENEFITS. Investing in open space can save communities money by reducing infrastructure and public service costs associated with sprawling development.[4]

ECONOMIC BENEFITS. Home buyers and businesses alike are attracted to open space amenities. In fact, recreation, parks, and open space are ranked as top priorities for relocating businesses.[5]

INFRASTRUCTURE BENEFITS. Considerable benefits can be gained by concentrating growth near areas of existing infrastructure while preserving key land and water resources. Acquisition of open space that protects drinking water, in particular, can save significant water treatment costs. Greenways that include bicycle paths and walkways also provide benefits by expanding a community's transportation network.

FLOOD PREVENTION BENEFITS. It is cheaper and easier to rehabilitate flood-damaged ballfields, playgrounds, and greenways than housing and commercial districts.

HEALTH AND ENVIRONMENTAL BENEFITS. Conserving open space is often the cheapest way to safeguard drinking water, clean the air, and achieve other public health and environmental goals.

COMMUNITY BENEFITS. The value of open space is often beyond measure, strengthening neighborhoods, building community, and preserving a sense of place. Parks and open space can also stabilize and revitalize distressed communities, stimulate commercial growth, and provide young people with constructive alternatives to crime and delinquency.[6]

protect their land and water resources, their community character, and their quality of life. The federal and state governments are also stepping up support for local efforts, providing new funding, tools, and incentives. Against this backdrop, open space protection has emerged as a sensible and cost-effective landuse planning tool—a voluntary approach that is an equal partner with regulation, zoning, and planning techniques.

The Preservation Project of Jacksonville, Florida, is one of the nation's most ambitious land conservation programs targeted at guiding growth and preserving access to nature. Unveiled in January 1999 by Mayor John Delaney, chief executive of the consolidated jurisdictions of Jacksonville and Duval County, the project is an ambitious, five-year, $312 million effort to acquire for public use approximately 10 percent of the city's remaining developable land—between 10 and 20 square miles—while improving access to the St. John's River and other natural areas. Several dozen city parks will also be upgraded.[7]

The Preservation Project uses land conservation as a growth management tool, targeting lands that are important in the effort to limit sprawl and contain growth, preserve environmentally sensitive areas, protect water quality and water resources, and expand public access. The project is part of the mayor's multibillion-dollar approach to growth management, trans-portation, the environment, and economic development called the Better Jacksonville Plan.

A variety of local, federal, and private conservation funding sources are being secured. Voters also approved an increase in the county sales tax to fund the Better Jacksonville Plan. Fifty million dollars of sales tax revenue is being directed to the Preservation Project. During the program's first three years, the city protected nearly 22,000 acres.

Florida provides strong support for local greenprinting programs like the one in Jacksonville. Florida Forever is among the most well-funded state land conservation programs in the country, and one with significant resources dedicated to urban land protection efforts like those in Jacksonville. Jacksonville was also able to draw on the experiences of other Florida counties that have had conservation programs in place for many years.

Greenprinting is a three-step process that begins with a vision: people identify the natural, cultural, and historical places that define their community and sustain their heritage. This vision may address multiple conservation and growth-related chal-lenges at the local or regional levels, from watershed protection, to brownfield redevelopment, to farmland preservation. Whatever the priorities, the key is to steer growth toward existing infrastructure and create natural corridors for conservation that connect protected lands.

Securing funds to implement the vision is the next step and the topic of this handbook. Most communities have a variety of funding sources available to them at the federal, state, private, and local levels. *Explore them all.* By securing funds from different sources, your community can create a "funding quilt" that is steady and sufficient to implement the greenprinting vision. Without funding diversity, you risk reliance on a single, potentially unpredictable funding source.

Each funding source is important. But keep in mind that federal, state, and private funds will probably act as supplements or incentives to the local share. Local funding is critical to your success. As such, the passage of a voter-approved conservation finance measure is the primary focus of this handbook.

PHOTO BY KEN SHERMAN

MOUNTAIN ISLAND LAKE AND ITS TRIBUTARIES PROVIDE DRINKING WATER FOR MORE THAN A MILLION PEOPLE IN METROPOLITAN CHARLOTTE, NORTH CAROLINA, AND SURROUNDING COUNTIES. VOTERS APPROVED A LAND ACQUISITION BOND IN NOVEMBER 1999 TO PROTECT THE WATERSHED.

With vision and funding in place, communities turn to the implementation phase of greenprinting, which involves acquiring and managing the land.

EXPLORING FEDERAL, STATE, AND PRIVATE CONSERVATION FUNDING SOURCES

Federal, state, and private funds are limited and in high demand. That means that the primary source of funding for a local greenprinting plan is usually a local government through a series of budget appropriations or through voter- or legislator-approved taxes and bonds. Outside funds can, however, serve as important supplements or incentives to local funding. The key is to examine all the options and design a strategy to secure available funds. By doing so, you can create a "funding quilt" that can sustain your greenprinting plan.

Federal funds are made available to state and local governments and nonprofit organizations through grants and incentives. Many of these programs require matching funds, underscoring the need to secure state, local, and private funds. (A summary of key federal conservation funding sources is located on page 10.) The availability of most federal conservation funds fluctuates annually depending on the political and economic climate. In 2002, Congress appropriated a record $1.6 billion for a variety of conservation programs and established a six-year federal commitment to these programs under the Conservation Spending Account. By setting up this account, Congress recognized the importance of ensuring a steady stream of funding for certain critical conservation programs.

States can play an enormous role in local greenprinting by putting forth an ambitious conservation vision and communicating this to local leaders. More and more states are also using conservation as a tool to manage and steer growth in their metropolitan areas.[8] Maryland has a long history of open space and farmland protection funded in part by a dedicated real-estate transfer tax. The state moved to link growth management and conservation in 1997 with passage of then-Governor Parris Glendening's smart-growth legislative package. The program designates priority funding areas where growth and conservation should occur. The initiative was followed in 2001 by Maryland's GreenPrint program which funds the protection of large tracts of priority land—identified as green infrastructure.

States can also provide local governments with two important funding tools: direct funding (grants and incentives) and the authority to raise local funds. Many states have significantly expanded these initiatives in recent years. (See page 12 for an evaluation of state conservation finance resources and tools.) New Jersey has been a national leader in land conservation since the launch of its Green Acres Program in 1961. In its first 40 years, a series of voter-approved bonds funded the protection of roughly 500,000 acres of open space and created hundreds of parks and recreation facilities. Counties and municipalities were given the authority to levy voter-approved property taxes to fund conservation with new enabling legislation in 1989. Then in 1998, state voters overwhelmingly approved the Garden State Preservation Trust Act, a constitutional amendment that dedicated one-tenth cent from state sales taxes for open space, generating $98 million annually for conservation.

Private funds from foundations, nonprofit land trusts, corporations, and individuals can also be an important boost to local or regional greenprinting initiatives. Foundations, in particular, have become increasingly active in the conservation and growth management arena, typically helping to fund national, regional, and local land trusts. Foundations can provide early funding and visioning support, helping communities leverage state and federal resources. In Kansas City, Missouri, the Hall Family Foundation worked with a team of planners and consultants on the first steps of MetroGreen, a regional greenway master plan that is designed to link seven metro counties. The foundation helped fund and direct the visioning process. The David and Lucille Packard Foundation is supporting greenprinting that protects the Lower Skagit River delta in Skagit County, Washington, from sprawl-related threats. The development of a comprehensive green-printing vision promotes smart-growth policies that protect natural resources and ecologically valuable land.

What is the most effective way to secure federal, state, and private funds? There is no one formula for success; funding can depend on the source, the program, the competition, and so on. There are, however, several steps worth considering:

DESIGN A GREENPRINTING PLAN. Many funders look for a well-designed and locally supported vision for conservation and growth before committing money. (Foundations can also become important visioning partners, assisting with the creation of your greenprinting plan.)

COMMIT LOCAL FUNDS. Local funding demonstrates local commitment and allows you to leverage private and other public funds.

RESEARCH FEDERAL, STATE, AND PRIVATE FUNDING PROGRAMS. Research existing funding sources at the federal, state, and private levels to determine where there is geographical or programmatic convergence. Look at programs that fund your community's specific greenprinting goals in other parts of the country, as well as grants that have been awarded to neighboring communities.

CREATE PARTNERSHIPS. Forge alliances with public and private sector leaders, such as state and federal elected officials and business, civic, and nonprofit leaders. These partners can help facilitate federal, state, and private funding and champion local efforts. Nonprofit land trusts, in particular, can be instrumental in helping to raise private funds from corporations and individuals. They can also solicit donations from foundations that may have policies against awarding grants directly to governmental agencies.

ESTABLISH A FOUNDATION. Contributors are often more comfortable donating to a foundation that supports a government project than to the government with the same mission.[9]

PHOTO BY KEN DUFALT

IN 1999, GOVERNOR JEB BUSH SIGNED THE FLORIDA FOREVER ACT. AUTHORIZED BY VOTERS AND PASSED BY THE LEGISLATURE, FLORIDA FOREVER DEDICATES $3 BILLION OVER TEN YEARS FOR THE ACQUISITION, RESTORATION, AND IMPROVEMENT OF RECREATION AND CONSERVATION LANDS.

Conservation foundations can facilitate new funding, raising money from individual and corporate donors, other foundations, and state and federal grant programs.

KEY FEDERAL CONSERVATION FUNDING SOURCES

Federal funds reach the local level directly or through administering state agencies. A summary of key federal conservation funding programs follows.

LAND AND WATER CONSERVATION FUND (LWCF). LWCF is the largest source of federal money for parks, wilderness, and open space acquisition. The program's funding comes primarily from offshore oil and gas drilling receipts. At the national level, funds are used to acquire and protect new national forests, parks, wildlife areas, and other public lands. In 2002, Congress appropriated $429 million for specific acquisitions in these federal units. The Land and Water Conservation Fund has a matching grant program that provides funds to states for planning, development, and acquiring land and water conservation areas. Following a five-year drought with no appropriations, Congress reinstated funding for the "stateside" program in 2000 and funded it at $144 million in 2002. Funds are apportioned annually to states on a formula basis.

THE FOREST LEGACY PROGRAM. This program is administered by the U.S. Forest Service under its State and Private Forestry division and provides matching funds to states to assist in forest protection. States may receive federal Forest Legacy grants of up to 75 percent of the total cost of the acquisition, with the remainder to be matched by nonfederal funds. In 2002, Congress appropriated $65 million for this program.

THE NORTH AMERICAN WETLANDS CONSERVATION ACT. This act promotes voluntary, public-private partnerships to conserve wetland ecosystems for waterfowl and other migratory birds. Acquired or restored habitat can be owned or managed by any federal, state, or nonprofit organization involved in land management. In 2002, Congress appropriated $43.5 million for this program.

THE COOPERATIVE ENDANGERED SPECIES CONSERVATION FUND. Section 6 of the Endangered Species Act provides matching grants to states for conservation projects that benefit candidate, proposed, and listed endangered species on state, private, and other nonfederal land. Congress appropriated more than $96 million for this program in 2002.

THE COASTAL ZONE MANAGEMENT PROGRAM (CZMP). CZMP, overseen by the National Oceanic and Atmospheric Administration, is a partnership between the federal government and 34 states and territories to better steward the nation's oceanic and Great Lakes coastline. While this program focuses primarily on management issues, there has been a recent push—backed by federal funding—to better integrate conservation within the overall management strategy for the coastal zone. The federal program requires each state to have its own coastal program, which brings in additional state funding.

THE FARMLAND PROTECTION PROGRAM. This program provides federal matching funds for state and local farmland protection efforts. To be eligible, a state, county, or local jurisdiction must have a complementary program of funding for the purchase of conservation easements. The recently enacted 2002 Farm Bill provides $600 million over six years for the Farmland Protection Program.

THE TRANSPORTATION EFFICIENCY ACT FOR THE 21ST CENTURY (TEA-21). TEA-21 provides states with funds to acquire land for historic preservation, trails, scenic beautification, and water-pollution mitigation related to surface transportation through its Transportation Enhancements program. The Recreational Trails Program provides funds for bike and pedestrian trails, and the Congestion Mitigation and Air Quality Improvement Program funds projects that improve air quality. TEA-21 was up for congressional reauthorization in 2003.

Additional funding is available through National Coastal Wetlands Conservation grants, the Wetlands Reserve Program, water-quality grants, and the Migratory Bird Conservation Fund.

STATE CONSERVATION FINANCE "BEST PRACTICES"

With state support, a local government has the tools and funding to realize its greenprinting vision. Without state support, local options are limited. While each state has its own unique history, laws, and approach to conservation funding, there are ways to evaluate a state's conservation finance landscape—the funding and the tools that provide the foundation for effective programs at the local level. The following framework was developed by the Trust for Public Land to encourage effective statewide support for local land conservation.

SUBSTANTIAL, DEDICATED STATE FUNDING SOURCE(S). A stable state revenue source is the foundation upon which effective conservation programs are built. States with dedicated funding sources (lotteries, sales taxes, general obligation bonds, and so on) are better able to foster program development and provide long-term conservation vision. Along with funding, states should establish time frames, demographic priorities, and targets for the number of acres to be protected. For example, the Florida Forever program provided $3 billion in state revenue bonds over ten years backed by the documentary stamp (real-estate transfer) tax. When the program was renewed by the legislature in 1999 and rechristened Florida Forever, funding for local governments and urban areas was greatly increased.

SIGNIFICANT LOCAL ENABLING OPTIONS. Federal and state governments cannot meet all local conservation needs. Therefore, states need to provide local governments with the legal authority to tax and dedicate revenues for land conservation (using property taxes, sales taxes, transfer taxes, bonding authority, and so on). In the process, local dollars and local control are expanded. Massachusetts, for instance, passed a law in 2000 that permits local referenda for the adoption of a property tax surcharge dedicated to open space protection, historic preservation, and affordable housing. Voters in 22 out of 45 communities approved Community Preservation Act measures in 2002.

A PROGRAM OF INCENTIVES FOR LOCAL GOVERN- MENTS. State incentives, often in the form of matching grants and low-interest loans, encourage local governments and nonprofit partners to generate local dollars while strengthening partnerships. New Jersey allows counties and towns to enact property tax–backed open space trust funds with voter approval. This funding is required for Green

Acres matching funds from the state. As of 2002, 19 of New Jersey's 21 counties and 144 of the state's 566 municipalities have established trust funds.

PURCHASE-OF-DEVELOPMENT-RIGHTS (PDR) PROGRAMS. PDR programs are a voluntary approach to conservation that allow for protection of the land combined with continued private ownership. To support the purchase of development rights, states can pass PDR enabling legislation, work cooperatively with local governments to purchase easements, appropriate funds to local governments and nonprofits, and create PDR programs that are administered at the state level.[10] California, Colorado, Maryland, Massachusetts, New Jersey, Pennsylvania, and Vermont all have state PDR programs.

PUBLIC-PRIVATE PARTNERSHIPS. Encouraging local governments to partner with private, nonprofit organizations can promote greenprinting goals, leverage conservation resources, and increase support for land conservation. Potential partners include land trusts, neighborhood and community groups, foundations, national conservation organizations, and landowner groups.

CONSERVATION TAX CREDITS. State tax credit laws are becoming an increasingly popular tool to encourage the donation of private land or easements to public or nonprofit entities for conservation. Such tax credits often receive strong support from private landowners and from those wary of outright public expenditures. Tax credit laws should be targeted to achieve state-specific conservation objectives—such as farmland conservation—without competing with broader funding sources. In 2001–02, new tax credit legislation was enacted in California, Colorado, Maryland, South Carolina, and Virginia.

SECURING LOCAL CONSERVATION FUNDS: TRENDS AND TECHNIQUES

No matter how much money you raise from federal, state, and private sources, considerable local funding is the key to effective, long-term conservation financing. Local funding means local commitment and local control—ingredients that can go a long way toward the implementation of a community's greenprinting vision. Local funds can also leverage federal, state, and private dollars, helping to establish a predictable and sizable conservation funding stream.

Local or regional conservation funding can take the form of a budget appropriation, tax increase, or bond issue by the legislative body. Often, however, the price tag, the politics, and the legal options demand approval by the voters, and such measures are the focus of this handbook. Ballot measures may be referred by the legislative body (termed a referendum) or placed on the ballot by citizen petition (termed an initiative). Some measures are advisory in nature, others create statutory obligations, and yet others may actually amend government charters. In New England, funding decisions can be made by residents at town meetings as well as on election day.

Voter approval for conservation is reaching record levels across the country: in 2002 alone, 74 percent of all state and local conservation measures were approved, generating roughly $5.7 billion in new public funding for parks and open space despite that year's economic recession and uncertain national security. The local ballot measures ranged in size from a $380,000 tax levy in the town of Buckland, Massachusetts (about half of which is dedicated to open space protection) to a $200 million, 10-year real-estate tax extension in Southampton, New York. State and local conservation measures generated nearly $1.7 billion in 2001 and $7.5 billion in 2002.[11]

Voters are clearly willing to spend money to protect their land and preserve their quality of life. They recognize that conservation is a wise investment that can pay significant dividends in the form of a safe environment, a strong economy, and a livable community.

Successful measures are the result of careful planning, hard work, and an understanding of public priorities. The process involves an assessment of public opinion about conservation and taxation and the design of a measure that is, as political consultant and TPL veteran Steven Glazer explains below, *compelling, affordable,* and *accountable:*

> · The land preservation benefit must be viewed by voters as a *compelling need.* Whether it addresses water quality protection, farmland preservation, or urban parks and playgrounds, proponents must understand voters' priorities and what they consider a fundamental, compelling need.

> · The tax must be *affordable.* Voters have a specific taxing threshold, even to support benefits they find compelling. Find out how much voters are willing to spend (not what the ideal program would cost) and design your measure accordingly.

> · Voters must have confidence that those in charge of spending the money will be *accountable* and responsible. Fiscal safeguards written into a measure can assure

anxious voters that their tax dollars are being spent wisely. Safeguards include fiscal audits, administrative cost caps, citizen advisory committee reviews, and sunset clauses.

Once such a measure is designed, a good campaign must be conducted to build broad support from community leaders and organizations and to communicate the key benefits of the measure to undecided voters. "If a campaign has done its work well," notes Glazer, "the measure should have minimal opposition, and the focus of the public debate will be on the measure's benefits and accountability."[12]

So how do you design a measure that is compelling, affordable, and accountable? And how do you communicate its benefits to voters? The answer is careful research and polling, intelligent measure design, and sound campaign strategy. By following these steps, a community can secure the local support needed to fund a greenprinting vision.

10 WAYS TO INCREASE
OPEN SPACE FUNDS

TPL's Conservation Finance Program created this "Top 10" list for land trusts that seek to generate new local and state funding for land conservation and other groups.

NUMBER 10. Take positions on public issues, advocate before public officials, and campaign for ballot measures—just as the American Red Cross, the Girl Scouts, and thousands of other 501(c)(3) charitable nonprofits do every day.

NUMBER 9. Know and follow the federal and state rules on lobbying and campaign finance. Recognize that, for instance, a land trust with an annual operating budget of $500,000 or less can spend up to 20 percent of its budget on lobbying for land conservation.

NUMBER 8. Learn what other land trusts are doing to increase public funding. Consult resources like LandVote (www.landvote.org), a service of TPL and the Land Trust Alliance.

NUMBER 7. Have a strategy that supports new and increased open space financing at the local and state levels. Be in the conservation finance business for the long run. Ballot campaigns and legislative advocacy are not one-time only or short-term pursuits.

NUMBER 6. Partner with other groups and individuals that seek increased public funding for land acquisition. Build coalitions to increase support and influence, and consider allying with business, agricultural, recreational, sporting, real estate, tourism, or other interests.

NUMBER 5. Know your legislators and other elected officials, and inform them of the benefits your land trust brings to the community and of the importance of actively protecting land.

NUMBER 4. Publicly endorse local ballot questions for open space funding. Be visible and tangible in your support of ballot measure campaigns. Collect signatures, organize phone banks, and donate resources like office space, computers, and copiers.

NUMBER 3. Encourage land trust members and volunteers to participate actively in legislative advocacy and ballot measure campaigns.

NUMBER 2. Donate land trust funds and encourage members and volunteers to contribute financially to ballot measure campaigns for open space funding.

NUMBER 1. Get and stay involved in public issues of land protection! Land trusts and their members are respected members of the community. Your leadership and credibility can influence elected officials and voters. Land trusts should lead on conservation finance, just as they do in transactions and stewardship. Be involved—in a responsible, accountable manner—in the issues of importance to land protection in your region!

NATIONAL TRENDS
IN CONSERVATION FINANCE

Voters have shown consistent support for conservation finance measures. The results of state and local measures across the country are provided here.

	1998	1999	2000	2001	2002
Measures Passed	126 (84%)	92 (90%)	174 (83%)	137 (70%)	139 (74%)
Billions Created	$8.3	$1.8	$7.5	$1.7	$5.7

AMERICANS VOTE TO PROTECT LAND

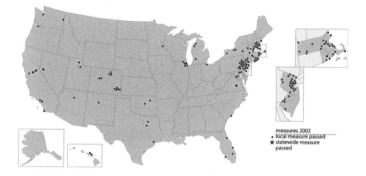

measures 2002
• local measure passed
★ statewide measure passed

SOURCE: LandVote, a service provided by the Trust for Public Land and the Land Trust Alliance. LandVote provides the nation's most comprehensive accounting of state and local ballot measures for parks and open space funding. Complete LandVote reports are available on-line at www.landvote.org.

■

CHAPTER TWO

Doing Your
Homework

Even Big Sky Country is not immune to suburban sprawl. In Gallatin County, Montana, subdivisions are quickly replacing family farms and ranches, transforming the valley's open landscape and undermining its agricultural heritage.

Several years ago, a citizens task force was appointed to stem this loss of land and preserve the community's quality of life. Task force members carefully examined a wide range of preservation options, both regulatory and incentives based. When public opinion polling showed strong support for a $10 million bond and a purchase-of-development-rights (PDR) program to protect the valley's open space, proponents launched a campaign. Voters approved the measure in November 2000, creating and funding Montana's first countywide PDR program.

Long before leaders in Gallatin County decided on a funding measure, drafted ballot language, or opened a campaign headquarters, they did their homework. Even if you have a good understanding of public policy and law and know your community well, you might be surprised at what you discover through the research and polling process. The Trust for Public Land routinely conducts research and polling—called feasibility assessment—before making recommendations on the design of a land conservation measure. Here are some typical questions:

· What are voters' top priorities, in general?

· Do voters generally support or oppose public spending measures?

· What is the public's opinion on such issues as growth, development, traffic, water quality, and the environment?

· What types of financing options are legally permissible and historically used, and how much will each raise?

· Is there public support for funding land conservation, and if so, how much are voters willing to spend?

· Within the context of land conservation, what are voters' top priorities?

· What is the process for designing a measure and putting it on the ballot?

Research is the first step toward passage of a conservation funding measure. Research will help you understand the community—its people, politics, economy, and voting patterns. Research will show you what is possible—the land conservation financing options and legal parameters for proposing a measure—and what has worked in your community and neighboring communities in the past. Finally, research will help you guide the polling process and design a measure that reflects conservation needs and public priorities.

Occasionally, proponents will decide, based on results of the research, that the time is not right to pursue a measure. For instance, voters may have rejected recent public spending measures at the ballot box. In other cases, economic and political indicators may suggest a more favorable outcome—or at least one that is worth testing in a public opinion poll.

This chapter describes the various components of thorough feasibility research. Chapter 3 covers public opinion polling, which is another part of this effort. Keep in mind that this process takes time. While the poll calls themselves can be completed in a couple of days, research and questionnaire design can take weeks or even months, depending on the scope of the project.

PHOTO BY PATRICIA ABOUSSIE

MORE THAN 17,000 ACRES OF GALLATIN COUNTY'S FARMLAND AND RANCHLAND HAVE BEEN DIVIDED FOR DEVELOPMENT IN THE LAST DECADE.

RESEARCHING BASIC DEMOGRAPHICS AND LANDUSE

The first step is to find out precisely who lives and votes in your community. It may sound simple, and you may think you know, but demographic patterns are constantly in flux and many communities are quickly changing. Check out the population and how it is changing by assessing rates of growth, population distribution, ethnicity, age, and education level. Your local, regional, and state planning agencies or the U.S. Census will have this information.

It is equally important to assess the strength of the local economy and related political issues. Economic growth, unemployment, and income trends can affect public and political support for new land conservation spending. This information can be particularly useful for the pollster and other professionals you might be hiring if they are not from the area. Sources for economic information may include your local, regional, or state economic development departments, the chamber of commerce, and newspaper archives.

RESEARCH CHECKLIST: COMMUNITY PROFILE

To create a demographic and landuse profile of your community, research the following:

DEMOGRAPHICS
- Population and growth rate
- Ethnicity, age, and education level
- Population distribution within jurisdiction
  (largest counties or municipalities)

ECONOMY
- Unemployment rate and trends
- Economic growth
- Major employers and industries
- Cost of living, median income, and median home price

ENVIRONMENT
- Landuse characteristics
- Agriculture, tourism, fishing, forestry, grazing, and mining industries
- Drinking water source and related land conservation issues
- Growth management issues
- Current environmental issues and concerns
- Statewide and local land conservation legislation and issues

Finally, it is essential to understand the issues that impact the quality of life in your community. Find out how growth is being managed and how it is impacting the community. Also assess any environmental, landuse, and land conservation issues that the community is addressing. An understanding of the inter-relationship of land conservation, the environment, and quality-of-life issues can result in a more informed public opinion poll and a stronger conservation measure.

INVESTIGATING FINANCING OPTIONS

Thorough fiscal research is an essential undertaking designed to help you understand the type and amount of public funds available for land conservation. By investigating the local economy and public spending trends, you'll also have a context for a potential bond measure or dedicated tax increase: you'll know not only what is possible but what is prudent.

Research can uncover the various financing options available, and public opinion polling can determine the level of support for each. It is important to consider all the options, not just those a community has used in the past. Available options depend on state and local laws and the current taxing capacity of your community. Some common approaches include sales taxes, property tax levies, bonds, and real estate transfer taxes. Each funding source has its own advantages and disadvantages and varying levels of support within a community. (See the table on page 29–31 for more information.)

The primary types of funding approaches are pay-as-you-go, long-term borrowing, or a combination of the two. With pay-as-you-go, government spends revenues from general appropriations or a dedicated funding source. These funding sources, which can include property assessments, sales tax set-asides, real-estate transfer taxes, and even onetime environmental fines and budget surpluses, can be attractive to debt-resistant voters and public officials.[13] Pay-as-you-go means year-by-year accountability and no borrowing costs. On the downside, it may also mean relatively small annual revenues (sometimes too small to pay for large projects), and its funding can be difficult to sustain if the politics of a community changes.

Long-term borrowing options present their own set of opportunities and obstacles. On the one hand, borrowing can provide a community with substantial revenue and the flexibility to fund large-scale park and open space projects, the costs of which are lower today than they will be tomorrow. There are, however, additional costs and financing charges associated with borrowing. In addition, bonds typically require voter approval—sometimes by supermajority levels—and convincing voters of the merits of incurring debt can be challenging. Finally, there is generally stiff competition for general obligation bonds among many local programs in need of financing. (For a more detailed look at conservation financing options, refer to TPL's *Local Parks, Local Financing, Volume I: Increasing Public Investment in Parks & Open Space*. Ordering information is available in the bibliography.)

CRUNCHING THE NUMBERS

As an example of your research, let's say that a local sales tax option exists in your community. You need to find out a variety of things about that tax before you test it in a poll or consider it as a conservation funding option. Some key questions:

· How much sales-taxing capacity remains?
Can the remaining tax be used for land conservation?

· In what increments (one-half cent, one-quarter cent, one-eighth cent, and so on) can the tax be imposed?

· What is the process (voter or legislative approval) by which a tax increase can be imposed?

· How much revenue can each taxing increment raise?

· What is the sales tax rate in neighboring jurisdictions?

· Have recent tax increase measures in the community been successful?

Once you've answered these questions, investigate the next option, such as a property tax levy.

A thorough fiscal analysis will help you determine which taxes and bonds can be levied and the cost of various tax increases to taxpayers. These amounts will be tested in the poll to determine the specific taxing level acceptable to voters. Critical components of this fiscal analysis include the following:

· An overview of potential land conservation funding sources

· An assessment of current taxes levied and trends in the tax base

· Taxing capacity and cost per household of a conservation tax increase

· Bonded indebtedness (the amount of debt incurred by a jurisdiction), debt ceilings (the maximum amount of debt allowed), and bond rating (the measurement that indicates the jurisdiction's likelihood of default)

· Spending priorities of the jurisdiction, including park and conservation-related dollars

In addition to determining the figures, check out recent levels of public spending on conservation and other areas. This will help you put a new financing measure in the context of overall public spending trends.

A variety of sources can be useful during the fiscal research process. The state department of revenue or state associations of cities or counties may have reports that detail taxing options, uses, limits, and so forth. Check as well with other jurisdictions that have used creative approaches. State statutes can provide the details of each option. A review of the jurisdiction's budget, comprehensive annual financial report, or audit will provide the local numbers.

It is also important to keep in mind that the design and implementation of a financing option may be complex, and legal counsel is often recommended.

RESEARCH CHECKLIST:
FINANCING OPTIONS

To determine the options for raising local conservation funds in your community, research the following:

FISCAL PORTRAIT
- Current taxes levied
- Trends in tax base
- Bonded indebtedness, debt ceilings, and bond rating
- Local and state budget issues
- Park and conservation agency budget and current funding sources
- Competing priorities for public funds

REVENUE OPTIONS
- Constitutional and statutory provisions
- Legislative history on revenue option reforms
- New versus existing revenue sources, and related bonding options
- Revenues used by similar jurisdictions
- Amounts raised by alternate tax levels
- Enactment process (referendum, initiatives, and so on)

COMMON LOCAL
FINANCING OPTIONS

PAY-AS-YOU-GO OPTIONS

METHOD
Property tax

DEFINITION
Tax on real property paid for by commercial and residential property owners

PROS
· Steady source of revenue
· Relatively easily administered
· Tax burden fairly broadly distributed
· Small increases create substantial funding
· Popular with voters when focused on compelling land conservation needs

CONS
· Competition for other public purposes
· Overall concern among taxpayers about high rates

METHOD
Sales and use tax

DEFINITION
Tax on the sales of goods or services

PROS
· Relatively easily administered
· Low reporting costs
· Can generate large sums, even at small tax levels
· Can tap into tourism profits generated by open space amenities
· May include exemptions such as food and medicine

CONS
· Revenues can drop when economy slows
· Considered regressive

METHOD
Real estate transfer tax

DEFINITION
Tax on the sale of property, paid by either the buyer or seller

PROS
· Funds can be substantial
· Nexus between taxing new development and protecting open space

CONS
· Opposition from real estate/development interests that makes passage difficult for some communities
· Less predictable revenue stream

COMMON LOCAL
FINANCING OPTIONS
(CONTINUED)

PAY-AS-YOU-GO OPTIONS

METHOD	DEFINITION
Impact fee	One time fee paid by developer to offset costs of infrastructure caused by new development

PROS
· Nexus between taxing new development and protecting open space

CONS
· Parks and open space projects might require direct link to new development
· May make housing development unaffordable

METHOD	DEFINITION
Special assessment	Special tax district for area that benefits from an open district space project

PROS
· Users finance acquisition and management
· Predictable revenue stream
· Accountability in government spending
· Sense of ownership of and responsibility for area parks and services
· Can establish in small increments
· May be able to set own election date and process

CONS
· Possibly time consuming to implement
· Overall concern among taxpayers about high rates

METHOD	DEFINITION
Business improvement district	Special tax district that assesses business owners for special services

PROS
· Same as special assessment district (see above)

CONS
· Same as special assessment district (see above)

METHOD	DEFINITION
General obligation bond	Loan taken out by a city or county against the value of the taxable property

PROS
- Allows for immediate purchase of open space, locking in land at current prices
- Distributes the cost of acquisition over time

CONS
- Extra interest costs of borrowing
- Voter approval often required, sometimes by supermajority levels

METHOD	DEFINITION
Revenue bond	Loan paid from proceeds of a tax levied for the use of a specific public project, or with proceeds of fees charged to those who use the financed facility

PROS
- Not constrained by debt ceilings of general obligation bonds
- Voter approval rarely required

CONS
- More expensive than general obligation bonds

CASE STUDY: CONSERVATION FINANCE RESEARCH EXAMINES FUNDING OPTIONS

TPL explored the options for funding conservation in a New Mexico community. The potential revenues, impact on taxpayers, and implementation process were examined.

SOURCE
Property tax

WHO PAYS
Property owners

REVENUE-GENERATING POTENTIAL
Property tax revenues generate about $500,000 annually. There is $600,000 in additional property-taxing capacity.

Potential Revenue	Tax Increase	Average Cost to Taxpayers*
$100,000	$0.84	$40

IMPLEMENTATION PROCESS
Voter approval is required for non operational purposes such as open space acquisition.

COMMENTS
Town approved a property tax levy for open space in 1999.

SOURCE
General obligation bond

WHO PAYS
Town incurs debt that is payable from property tax receipts.

REVENUE-GENERATING POTENTIAL
Property tax revenues generate about $500,000 annually. There is $600,000 in additional property-taxing capacity.

Bond**	Average Annual Cost to Taxpayers*
$1 million	$30
$2 million	$60

IMPLEMENTATION PROCESS
Voter approval is required.

COMMENTS
Maximum bonding capacity is $5 million (limited to 4 percent of the town's net taxable value). Currently no general obligation bonds outstanding.

SOURCE
Sales tax

WHO PAYS
Businesses (although cost is typically passed on to consumers)

REVENUE-GENERATING POTENTIAL
A sales tax of 1/8 percent (0.125) may be levied. The tax may be levied in increments of 1/16 percent (0.0625) in separate ordinances. This is the only remaining sales-taxing capacity available to the town.

Tax	Potential Annual Revenue
1/16 percent	$375,000
1/8 percent	$750,000

IMPLEMENTATION PROCESS
Any portion of the new taxing authority (1/8 percent) requires majority voter approval. If the measure fails, one year must pass before the question is submitted again.

COMMENTS
New sales tax revenues can be used for the acquisition of open space or to issue revenue bonds for such purpose.

SOURCE
Revenue bonds (sales tax backed)

WHO PAYS
Town incurs debt that is payable by sales tax revenues.

REVENUE-GENERATING POTENTIAL
There are no legal debt limits for revenue bonds. Current practice is for debt service to be between 15 percent and 20 percent of sales tax revenues. Town has outstanding revenue bonds representing about 16 percent of total sales tax revenues. New revenue bonds of about $1.5 million would increase the percentage to 20 percent of total sales tax revenues. Increasing the sales tax rate would allow for $1–$2 million in additional revenue bonds without increasing the current percentage of sales tax revenues to debt.

IMPLEMENTATION PROCESS
Ordinance must be approved by at least two-thirds of the council or it is subject to an election.

COMMENTS
None

---

*cost to owners of a $150,000 home
**assumes 20-year bonds, compounded annually at 5.5 percent interest

RESEARCHING LEGAL CONSTRAINTS

The steps for getting a measure on the ballot vary from state to state and community to community. Carefully research all the possibilities; this information is essential for the poll and the measure design process. And remember, there is no such thing as a minor legal error. Any mistake in following filing requirements, signature forms, ballot wording, or other rules can kill a measure, so hire or get pro bono experienced legal counsel. A jurisdiction's counsel and/or outside legal counsel should be relied on to assist with this process.

You may want to think of the legal research in terms of *who, what, when,* and *how much:*

> · *Who* can place a measure on the ballot, either legislatively (referendum) or by citizen petition (initiative)? What are the requirements for each approach?

> · *Who* handles measure preparation and approval (county attorney, county clerk, and so on)? *Who* else can have input into this process (citizen activists, community groups, and so on)?

> · *What* can the measure look like? Review laws and regulations for ballot title, wording, and arguments. It is helpful to consider ballot language for past fiscal and environmental measures to see what's possible and what has and hasn't worked well. *What* are the public notice requirements for the measure?

> · *When* are ballot measures permitted (for example, in general and special elections but not primaries)? *When* are the deadlines for placing a measure on the ballot?

· *How much* support is needed (simple majority voter approval, two-thirds, and so on)? Is a minimum voter turnout required?

Getting the measure on the ballot is just one part of the legal equation. Election law is the next. Before you launch a campaign to pass a measure, you must understand the rules governing the establishment of a campaign committee, reporting contributions and expenditures, and many other details. (See page 94 for a complete review of campaign legal issues.)

In November 1992, Los Angeles County voters approved Proposition A, the Safe Neighborhood Parks Act, generating $540 million for park acquisition and improvements, beach and recreation facilities, at-risk youth and gang prevention programs, stream and river restoration, trail construction, and tree planting. To create the largest assessment district in the state, campaign leaders assembled two distinct legal teams. The first team advised on the drafting of state legislation that was necessary to create the district and reviewed the legal aspects of the engineer's report and

PHOTO BY MATT O'BRIEN

LOS ANGELES RESIDENTS HAVE APPROVED SEVERAL PARK AND OPEN SPACE BOND MEASURES SINCE THE 1990S. CITY LEADERS ARE NOW LAUNCHING A GREENPRINTING LOS ANGELES INITIATIVE THAT IS DESIGNED TO IDENTIFY AND CREATE OPPORTUNITIES AND FUNDING FOR CONSERVATION.

the proposed assessment rate and method. The second legal team provided election advice, making sure the campaign was in accordance with election and financial reporting requirements.

"We were very careful to ensure detailed legal review of our enabling legislation and ballot measure by county counsel as well as by outside counsel with expertise in assessment case law, forming assessment districts, issuing assessment bonds, and litigating assessments," reported campaign director Esther Feldman about Proposition A. "Assessment law is quite complex, and adequate and early legal review is vital to minimize the risks of legal challenges and potentially costly or fatal mistakes."[14]

It is important to note that public agencies may spend time and resources to research and design a ballot measure. Once a measure is on the ballot, however, these entities are barred from conducting any type of campaign activity.

RESEARCH CHECKLIST:
LEGAL ISSUES AND CONSTRAINTS

To determine the legal issues and constraints in your community, research the following:

- Schedule of elections at which ballot measures are permitted
- Requirements for placing a measure on the ballot
- Requirements for ballot language
- Procedure for measure preparation and approval
- Use of ballot arguments
- Public notice requirements
- Examples of previous ballot titles, language, and arguments
- Rules for establishing a campaign committee and for reporting contributions and expenditures

ANALYZING ELECTION DATA

Voters in one Midwestern community passed 70 percent of all fiscal measures in the late 1990s—tax levies for schools, infrastructure bonds, even a conservation spending measure. That is good information to have, but it is not enough. A closer look at past election results reveals that nearly all of the winning measures were placed on general election ballots (elections that attracted a high percentage of registered voters). All the losing measures were on special election ballots.

While every community and every election is unique, certain highly motivated voting groups can have disproportionate influence in special elections (for example, parents in a school board race). Identifying these trends can help you make an informed choice about the timing of your measure.

An analysis of the specific political landscape and election trends will help you understand voting behavior in your community. Use this information to map out your political strategy and draft your poll questions.

Begin with a look at the success of all fiscal and environmental measures in a community over the past five years. Assessing how well these measures have fared at which elections (special, primary, general, or mail ballot) and comparing these data with voter turnout figures can help you determine which measures have the best chance of winning at what time. Election results and turnout figures can be obtained from your local election department or board of elections; a review of newspaper coverage can also provide important background on campaigns, ballot measures, and politics that have influenced the results.

Take an even closer look at previous attempts to pass land conservation–funding measures or spending measures of similar sizes. Look beyond the vote result: How visible was the campaign? What were the main issues or controversies? How much money was spent on the campaigns?

Election research helped local leaders in Ocean County, New Jersey, assess potential support for a conservation finance measure. Since state enabling legislation was passed in 1989, counties and municipalities across New Jersey have created property tax–backed open space trust funds with voter approval. Initially, leaders in fast-growing Ocean County were reluctant to make the attempt. Many members of the solidly Republican county legislature—Board of Chosen Freeholders—were committed to keeping taxes low, and the county's large senior citizen population was considered unlikely to support new taxes for land conservation. Yet an analysis of voting patterns on statewide Green Acres bond measures showed solid support from those precincts with higher-than-average proportions of seniors. Polling confirmed these results: a respected

RESEARCH CHECKLIST:
ELECTION ANALYSIS

To create a political profile of your community, research the following:

- · Overview of local politics
- · Voter registration (how to register, current registration by party)
- · Voter turnout, including analysis of turnout rates and projections for future ballots (consider all potentially applicable ballots: general, primary, and special)
- · Voting history on key races (president, governor, senators, and U.S. representative; city, county, and state fiscal and environmental measures; local elected officials; similar measures in nearby jurisdictions)
- · Down-ballot drop-off rates for ballot measures: what is the voter turnout for conservation measures listed down on the ballot versus the turnout for the major candidate races listed first?
- · Background on selected races (campaign issues, contributions and expenditures, visibility of the race, key supporters, endorsements, opposition, and pro-and-con arguments)
- · Listing of key environmental and community leaders
- · Poll results from surveys conducted by government agencies, nonprofits, or other entities. Results may help illuminate voter opinions about local politics, finances, landuse, and so on
- · Written statements and other commentary on the issue of land conservation from public officials, community leaders, and interested parties

local Republican polling firm found that seniors and Republicans favored the trust fund and a reasonable tax levy by a solid margin. In November 1997, Ocean County became one of 13 New Jersey counties and 53 municipalities to establish an open space trust fund. The fund raises roughly $4 million a year to protect the region's watershed and agricultural lands.

LOCAL ELECTION ANALYSIS

It is easy to spot trends when election results and voter turnout figures are put into graphs. The results from this county show that financing measures succeed most often in high-turnout, general elections. Test this result further in your poll by comparing levels of support among high-propensity and low-propensity voters.

VOTER TURNOUT—1998–2002

This graph measures voter turnout in all types of elections held in the county over a five-year period.

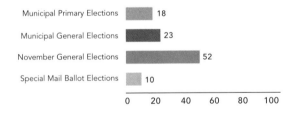

ELECTION RESULTS OF FISCAL MEASURES—1998–2002

This graph measures the success rate of fiscal measures over a five-year period. Municipal, county, special district, and state measures are included.

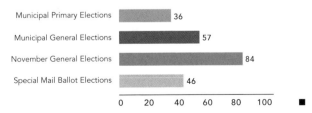

CHAPTER THREE

Measuring
Public Opinion

Two states, four counties, and one city all working together to create and fund joint regional park districts over a span of 40 miles on both sides of the Mississippi River: sound ambitious? Organizers of the effort to form regional park districts in the St. Louis metro area thought so, but it didn't deter them from trying. These leaders, headed by former U.S. Senator John C. Danforth of Missouri and St. Louis 2004 president Peter Sortino, envisioned an interconnected park and open space system that would be funded and managed cooperatively by regional park districts in Illinois and Missouri. The project is part of St. Louis 2004, a series of civic projects undertaken to celebrate the bicentennial of the Lewis and Clark expedition setting out from that city, as well as the 100th anniversary of the 1904 World's Fair.

A project of this magnitude required a thorough examination of public priorities, fiscal options, and legal constraints. Extensive community outreach and expert polling were essential. Results from the first public opinion poll conducted in late 1998 demonstrated strong public support for a sales tax and for programs that improve water quality, provide community trails and wildlife habitat, repair existing parks, and provide public access to natural areas. This poll gave organizers the information they needed to design park district enabling legislation (required in both states) and to create uniform ballot measures in each local jurisdiction.

The result from the poll was Proposition C, the Clean Water, Safe Parks and Community Trails initiative.

Once the measures were on the ballot, a second "campaign" poll was conducted to help organizers guide the public education effort and allocate campaign resources effectively. Prop C had among its critics those who were wary of a new level of bureaucracy unaccountable to voters. But the measure was well designed and reflective of public priorities, and the campaign was well organized. After years of planning, voters in four counties and the City of St. Louis approved Prop C in November 2000.

Whether you are launching a multijurisdictional, regional initiative or a small-town conservation ballot measure, a public opinion poll is almost always money well spent. A professional, scientific public opinion poll can help you chart your course from the design of a measure through election day. Consider what a well-designed, well-executed poll can tell you:

- Valuable information about whether a measure can win and how much new taxing and/or spending voters will accept

- The public's conservation priorities, for example, the protection of wildlife habitat, expanded parks and playgrounds, and the preservation of farmland

- Objective data necessary to design a conservation ballot measure, build political support, and launch a winning campaign

However, without careful research and the guidance of a professional pollster and political consultant, polls can mislead as much as guide your efforts. This chapter looks at some key considerations for successful polling and shows ways to make

SOURCE: STEARNS CONSULTING

POLLING HELPED PROPONENTS OF PROPO-
SITION C IN ST. LOUIS WAGE A SUCCESSFUL
CAMPAIGN FOR SAFE CITY PARKS.

sure the poll accurately reflects the sentiment of the voters.
While the pollster you hire will direct the polling process, it is
up to you to keep him or her on track. Understanding the
fundamentals of polling is essential.

Keep in mind that a poll is only a snapshot of voter sentiment
at the time the survey is conducted. Current events can change
voter attitudes, and polls do not predict future behavior. Also,
while polls are valuable tools for shaping a conservation finance
measure, they are only one of many sources of information you
will need to consider. Ultimately, your measure should reflect
public priorities and be guided by sound public policy.

INTERVIEWING COMMUNITY LEADERS

Interviews with community leaders will help guide the design
of your poll. These interviews serve two purposes. First, they

CASE STUDY: SURVEY REVEALS COMMUNITY'S CONSERVATION PRIORITIES

POLL TYPE: Ballot measure design

JURISDICTION: Forest Preserve District of Kane County, Illinois

DATE: December 1998

SAMPLE SIZE: 400

MARGIN OF ERROR: +/-4.9 percent

POLLSTER: American Viewpoint

BACKGROUND: Largely suburban with a strong agricultural base, Kane County, outside Chicago, experienced a 27 percent increase in population in the last decade. To protect natural resources and quality of life, the Forest Preserve District made the acquisition of open space a top priority. The district worked with the Conservation Foundation, a regional nonprofit land and water protection organization, and the Trust for Public Land to secure funds for land acquisition.

POLL OBJECTIVE: The primary objective of the poll was to test public opinion about a proposed measure to fund open space acquisition by the Forest Preserve District.

KEY FINDINGS:
- Support for a $70 million general obligation bond was strong, increasing further when voters heard the arguments for and against the measure.
- Voters agreed strongly that protecting open space lands—such as greenways, bike paths, and forest preserve—plays a very important role in preserving the quality of life and stopping urban sprawl.
- Voters also felt a sense of urgency: with land prices on the rise and open space dwindling, land must be protected for children and for future generations.
- The protection of land to improve air and water quality was a top priority.
- Voters responded well to the guarantee of an annual, independent audit of bond funds.

SAMPLE QUESTION: "Now I would like to tell you some of the ways in which the Forest Preserve District may use the funds from the bond referendum. Do you approve or disapprove of the following . . . "
Voters responded to a list of potential uses for the bond money, including acquisition of neighborhood parkland, bike paths and trails, greenways, and a family campground. The results of these questions indicated strong support for the following conservation issues: the protection of forests and planting of trees to improve air quality; the protection of watershed land

that can improve the quality of rivers and streams; the improvement of trails, fishing access, and other recreational areas; the enhancement of flood control efforts; and educational programs for children and adults. These conservation priorities were included in the ballot measure.

BALLOT LANGUAGE: "Shall the Forest Preserve District of Kane County, Illinois, borrow money and issue general obligation bonds in an amount not to exceed $70 million in order to improve existing forest preserves, wetland, and prairies; and to acquire and preserve forests and natural lands that will improve air and water quality, protect wildlife habitat, enhance flood control protection, expand public access to hiking and biking trails, fishing and other recreational areas, and provide forest and wildlife educational programs for children and families, all in accordance with the purposes authorized by the Downstate Forest Preserve District Act of the State of Illinois as amended, and with all expenditures subject to an annual independent audit?"

USE OF POLL RESULTS: Poll results were used to gauge public support for a measure, determine the most appropriate funding amount, and assess land conservation priorities.

IMPACT: Voters approved a $70 million land conservation measure in 1999.

provide insight into current events, public spending patterns, behind-the-scenes politics, and land conservation priorities. In addition, the interviews themselves help assure community leaders that the polling process is inclusive and that their perspectives are being considered.

Typically, the Trust for Public Land conducts interviews with a group of community leaders and public officials or an established citizens advisory committee. The interviews roughly follow the outline of the research topics in chapter 2 (see pages 24 and 26): community priorities, financing options, land conservation and environmental issues, and so on. Be careful, however, not to get bogged down in technical questions; focus instead on the person's opinions about various conservation possibilities. A listing of community survey questions follows.

· What are the arguments for increasing public funding for parks and open space?

· What are the arguments against increasing public funding for parks and open space?

· What would be the most popular things a park and open space funding measure could pay for? The least popular?

· What other priorities might be linked to conservation: for example, watershed protection, containment of sprawl, economic opportunities (possible linkages to tourism and recreation industry), and others?

· Who are the most prominent and credible groups and individuals, including public officials, who might support or oppose a parks and open space funding measure?

· Are there any controversies about the environment, landuse, or the local government that could affect a park and open space measure?

· What other public spending needs might be a priority with voters?

The number of interviews conducted depends on the core group assembled. The selection of written or oral questionnaires also varies depending on the needs of the participants.

SELECTING A POLLSTER

The pollster is responsible for designing a public opinion poll, selecting the sample, conducting the survey, and interpreting the results. Just how well this is done and how much help you get along the way can vary considerably. There are many good pollsters who have experience with successful conservation finance measures. Look for a nationally respected polling firm or an experienced regional pollster who has been recommended by local partners and government officials. These firms often have special expertise and/or knowledge of the community that is useful to the process. Here is a summary of some things to consider:

· Find someone who is professional and has experience, preferably with environmental and/or conservation ballot measures.

· Find someone who is willing to provide advice throughout the campaign, from designing the ballot measure to reviewing direct mail pieces. Notes one nationally respected polling firm: "a good pollster does not just deliver a pile of numbers but helps you turn those numbers into effective messages."[15]

· Check the firm's references, find out how many other clients it has, and determine who will be your principal contact.

· Outline the agreement in a written contract.

Prices can vary considerably depending on the pollster, the size of the sample, and the length of the questionnaire. A well-designed land conservation finance poll can range from $10,000 to $13,000 for a 15-minute poll with a sample size of 300, and up to $30,000 for a 20-minute poll with a sample size of 800. (As a general guideline, a poll should have a sample size of at least 300 to get an acceptable margin of error, and 400 is much better. If information about various voter subsets is vital, the sample size should be even larger.)

Once the results are in, your pollster will help you interpret them and recommend how to target voters and craft key messages for your campaign. Depending on your contract with the pollster, here is generally what you can expect once the survey is complete:

TOP-LINES. Top-lines are the overall results to the poll questions.

CROSS-TABS. Cross-tabs allow you to see how different groups of voters responded to a question. For example, a cross-tab will show the results of an initial and secondary ballot test crossed by gender, age, location, and so on. This information gives you the ability to identify base, swing, and opposition voters and to determine which messages resonate with each group. The pollster will provide you with a set of cross-tabs, but you can also ask for additional breakouts if necessary.

POLL ANALYSIS. A good pollster will help you interpret the results by providing a written analysis of the responses. This report should include strategic recommendations.

Keep in mind that the materials and services provided by a pollster may vary. For example, a pollster may provide a written summary of results, targeting, and message as well as a full, question-by-question analysis. Pollsters will typically be available to brief campaign committees or staff about the results. Negotiate these and other needs with the pollster in advance.

CASE STUDY: BOISE SURVEY ASSESSES VOTERS' SPENDING TOLERANCE

POLL TYPE: Ballot measure design

JURISDICTION: Boise, Idaho

DATE: February 2001

SAMPLE SIZE: 400

MARGIN OF ERROR: +/- 5 percent

POLLSTER: Moore Information

BACKGROUND: Growth and development were threatening the foothills that surround the city of Boise. These foothills define the local landscape, provide recreational opportunities, and preserve quality of life. Led by former Mayor Brent Coles, a coalition of conservation-minded citizens explored the level of public support for open space protection funding in the Boise Foothills.

POLL OBJECTIVES: The objectives of the poll were to determine the taxing tolerance of voters for open space protection and to help assess conservation priorities within the Boise Foothills.

KEY FINDINGS:

· Growth and development, traffic, and congestion were top concerns among Boise voters, following only education.

· The protection of water quality, wildlife habitat, open space, and recreational opportunities were the most significant benefits that could be funded with an open space protection levy.

· Voters would support a tax levy for conservation as long as it wasn't too high.

· After voters heard positive and negative information during the poll, their support for a $10 million measure increased.

SAMPLE QUESTION: "The $10 million measure will cost Boise home-owners an additional $2.33 per month in taxes per year for each $100,000 of assessed home value. Knowing this, would you vote for or against the measure?"

Voters were initially split on whether to support the creation of a $10 million Foothills Open Space Protection Fund to be funded by a two-year property tax. Yet when voters were informed of what the tax would actually cost average homeowners each month, their level of support increased. These costs were included in the ballot summary.

BALLOT LANGUAGE: "For the purpose of preserving land in the Boise Foothills as open space and natural areas, shall the City of Boise establish a Foothills Open Space Protection Fund with a $5 million property tax override for each of two years, subject to a review by a citizens committee and an annual independent audit?"

BALLOT SUMMARY: "Proposed Open Space Protection Fund would acquire open space and natural areas in the Boise Foothills. Approved levy funds will:

· Protect water quality

· Preserve wildlife habitat

· Provide increased recreational areas for walking, biking, and other outdoor activities

· Limit over development and traffic

· Protect natural vegetation that prevents mudflows and washouts

Buying open spaces for public use will balance private development in the Boise area. Cost of the levy is $2.33/month for each one hundred thousand dollars of assessed home value, for two years only."

USE OF POLL RESULTS: Poll results were used to guide the design of the measure to reflect public priorities and spending tolerance.

IMPACT: Voters approved the $10 million conservation measure in May 2001 with 59 percent of the vote.

CONDUCTING THE RIGHT POLL AT THE RIGHT TIME

Typically, two types of polls are used for a conservation finance measure: a measure design poll and a campaign poll. The former guides the design of a measure, including ballot wording, spending amount, and land conservation priorities. This poll should be taken early—before a measure is designed or a decision is made to move forward. The latter guides the implementation of a campaign, revealing which information is most important to communicate to swing voters and testing shifts in voter attitudes.

DEFINITION OF POLLING TERMS

BASE VOTERS: Voters who strongly support a measure and are unmoved by arguments.

CROSS-TABS: Poll results provided for various subsets of voters. For example, results of a threshold question crossed by voter age, location, party, and responses to other questions.

MARGIN OF ERROR: A range of numbers that reflects a pollster's confidence in the results (usually expressed as "plus or minus X%"). The larger the sample size, the lower the margin of error.

SAMPLE: The voter group(s) selected as poll respondents.

SAMPLE SIZE: The total number of voters to be polled.

SUBSET: A defined group of voters within the sample. For example, women under age 40.

SWING VOTERS: Persuadable voters who either weakly support, weakly oppose, or are undecided on an issue.

TOP-LINES: The overall results to the poll questions.

Unfortunately, limited resources often preclude testing public opinion in more than one poll. In these cases, one comprehensive, carefully worded poll will determine both the elements of a measure and a campaign. If funds are limited, think carefully before you consider a second campaign poll close to election day. You may be looking for reassurance that you're on the right track or trying to assess the impact of a new development, but if the information is likely to come too late to change course, it is better to put your money into direct voter communications.[16]

DESIGNING AND INTERPRETING YOUR POLL

Ballot measure polls typically test voters' overall opinions about quality of life, spending priorities, and the performance of public agencies. They also test more detailed questions to

CASE STUDY: TWO POLLS HELP SHAPE
A MEASURE TO REFLECT PUBLIC PRIORITIES

On November 5, 1996, Miami-Dade County voters overwhelmingly approved a $200 million general obligation bond measure to fund capital improvements for park and recreation facilities. With 67 percent of the vote—the highest for a fiscal measure in the county's history—the Safe Neighborhood Parks Act brought the county and its municipalities together in a common cause: to demonstrate how parks and recreational programs can make a community safer and improve the quality of life of the residents who live there.

A full year before the measure reached the ballot box, proponents conducted a public opinion poll to determine park and recreation priorities and potential support for a park funding measure. The poll showed that crime (particularly juvenile violence), government mismanagement, and rampant growth and development were top public concerns. As a result, voters generally supported spending for juvenile crime prevention facilities, natural resources protection (including Biscayne Bay), the creation of safer neighborhood parks and facilities, and improving quality of life. Their spending tolerance: no more than $7 to $10 annually per household and no more than $200 million total.

The results of the survey helped proponents shape the early version of a bond measure, explore bond-financing scenarios, and work with park and recreation agencies to prioritize their needs in a way that reflected public concerns and priorities. The results were also helpful in securing early campaign funding and in gathering support from the county commissioners who would ultimately refer the measure to the ballot.

A second public opinion poll was conducted in spring of 1996. This poll served to further define the scope of the proposed measure and the strategy to secure its passage. The poll found that a targeted campaign that high-lighted specific park projects and their benefits would have the greatest chance of success. In fact, when participants were informed of the goals of the proposed projects—safety, conservation, juvenile crime prevention—support rose from 49 percent to 65 percent. The poll also helped proponents determine the strongest spokespeople, the most appropriate election date, swing voting groups and potential messages, and the importance of fiscal safeguards.

PHOTO BY ROBERT MCCLYMONDS

THE CAMPAIGN FOR MIAMI-DADE COUNTY'S SAFE NEIGHBORHOOD PARKS ACT SHOWCASED LOCAL PARK AND RECREATION PROJECTS AND SAFETY IMPROVEMENTS.

determine the degree of support and opposition to a measure, acceptable funding levels, pro-and-con arguments, the strength of competing measures, and potential endorsers. This section takes you through the types of questions your conservation poll should include and how to interpret the results.[17]

THE THRESHOLD QUESTION: CAN YOU WIN?

The threshold question of a poll is designed to assess voter support for a land conservation finance measure and to test whether support increases or decreases with more information. In a rough way, it mimics a campaign, first assessing what voters might do when they read the ballot language in the voting booth and then determining whether that level of support increases or decreases after communicating supporting and opposing messages to voters. For instance, a majority of voters may say early in the poll that they are inclined to reject a land conserva-tion funding measure. Once they have heard that the land protected will prevent sprawl and protect the quality of drinking water, however, their level of support may increase as shown by their answers to a follow-up question.

Test support for your measure twice, using actual ballot language whenever possible. The first question assesses the baseline level of support without any bias. After providing more information, including arguments for and against the measure, retest the level of support. Compare the numbers to determine which way voters are moving and look carefully at the cross-tabs to see which demographic groups are most influenced by which kinds of information about the measure. For example, a large number of women under age 50 may move from the undecided column to support a measure once they learn about the park improvements and safety elements. Alternatively, older voters may be inclined to reject a measure after hearing information about its impact on taxes.

The information from these threshold questions will help you decide whether it is possible to design a winning measure and how strong a campaign you'll need to move voters to your column. "Ballot measure campaigns require a lot of hard work, money, political capital, and expertise," notes conservation finance expert Corey Brown of the Big Sur Land Trust. "They burn up a tremendous amount of opportunity time. Winning is nearly everything. There is simply not enough time to waste on measures that cannot win," he explains.[18] Brown advises that it is probably best not to proceed if:

· The combined level of "strong support" (those voters who wholeheartedly endorse the measure) and "somewhat support" (less committed supporters) totals less than 50 percent of those persons polled; or

· The "strong oppose" (those firmly against the measure) is more than 35 percent; or

· The combined "strong oppose" and "somewhat oppose" (less committed opponents) is more than 45 percent.

Do proceed further if the combined "strong support" and "somewhat support" total is at least 60 to 65 percent, with at least 45 percent indicating strong support. If your support falls between the amounts listed above, base your decision on the following factors:

· Level of "strong support" and "strong oppose"

· Level of "somewhat support" and "somewhat oppose"

· Your ability to deliver messages that are persuasive with the key swing voter groups

· The amount of resources (for example, campaign funds, volunteers, editorial support) that you expect to be able to generate for the measure, with an emphasis on campaign fundraising

· Whether the measure will have opposition and, if so, the amount of resources the opposition will be able to allocate to defeat the measure

It is important to remember that these are not hard-and-fast rules and that they should be assessed in the context of the overall campaign.

HOW MUCH ARE VOTERS WILLING TO SPEND?

In November 1996, voters in the fast-growing community of Routt County, Colorado, approved a tax increase to purchase the development rights of its dwindling ranchlands, the first of its kind in the Rocky Mountain West. Despite initial hopes by community supporters for a higher levy, the poll clearly indicated voters' taxing threshold—between $9 and $25 a year for the average homeowner. This finding proved crucial to the measure's success and underscores the importance of polling, even in relatively low-budget campaigns like the one in Routt County.

It may be tempting to add up the cost of all the conservation projects you'd like to complete and then attach that number to your ballot measure. But you'll probably be wasting your time and money. Instead, use your poll to determine how much voters are willing to spend and then decide if that figure is worth the effort.

To determine the numbers, test both the overall amounts and their costs to individual taxpayers. For instance, the price of a measure might cost the average taxpayer $5, $10, $25, or $50 a year. Where do voters reach their spending limit, switching from support to opposition? This type of question was tested effectively in Ocean County, New Jersey, in 1997. When results of a poll showed public acceptance of $10 a year for open space instead of $20, the measure's price tag was reduced. More than 60 percent of voters supported the Ocean County Natural Lands Trust Fund measure. It is also important to discern how much money your swing voting blocks are willing to spend for a measure. For example, if you need strong support from senior citizens who are concerned about the cost of the measure, keep the price tag within comfortable limits.

In addition to testing dollar amounts, it is essential to test various financing options. Your research will tell you the options available to the jurisdiction, such as a general obligation bond or dedicated sales tax. The poll should ask which available financing options voters are most likely to support, presenting arguments for and against each one. For instance, a general obligation bond will limit a jurisdiction's future borrowing capacity and cost taxpayers interest, yet bonds allow land to be purchased now that might otherwise be unaffordable in years to come. These distinctions may be spelled out in a poll.

WHAT DO VOTERS WANT?

When it came to conservation, Santa Fe County voters gave top priority to the protection of historic and cultural sites. In DuPage County, Illinois, voters were concerned with acquiring open space to prevent sprawl and flooding. In Miami-Dade County, Florida, the creation of safe parks and recreational programs to prevent juvenile delinquency ranked high. Each of these communities approved conservation finance measures that connected voters' concerns with the value of open space, demonstrating the importance of testing voter attitudes on a wide range of issues, not just the environment. Some questions might include: Is clean drinking water of most concern to voters? How wary are people of new government spending? Are crime, gangs, and drugs threatening the safety of a community? How are growth and development impacting a community? Knowing the answers to these questions and others like them can help you design a conservation measure with the broadest public support.

Your poll can help you design a measure that reflects public conservation priorities, such as protecting open space, preserving wildlife habitat, or increasing recreational programs. Your poll can also help you refine the communications you send about these priorities to targeted voters. For example, poll results may show that open space protection is a top priority. It may further reveal why open space protection is important to different groups: perhaps preventing urban sprawl and protecting land that preserves water quality are the top concern among voters age 40 and under, and public safety in parks scores highest for voters age 60 and older. Your campaign should target these specific messages to the appropriate groups. Study your cross-tabs carefully to determine which information moves which voters—Democrats, Republicans, Independents, women, men, seniors, younger voters, and so on. Then design your campaign strategy accordingly. (See chapter 5 for a detailed discussion of message development and the identification of swing voters.)

If your budget permits, testing potential arguments against your measure can be useful. Do people feel that taxes are already too high? Should funds be allocated to the management of existing land instead of the purchase of new land? By understanding opposition arguments, you can design a measure that addresses public concerns. For instance, if voters do not trust the government to spend their tax dollars wisely, include safeguards in your measure that ensure proper fiscal oversight. You may also find that the public simply needs better information about the type of lands that are threatened by development or the cost of land protection.

PHOTO BY TED HARRISON

VOTERS IN AUSTIN, TEXAS, HAVE APPROVED SEVERAL CONSERVATION FUNDING MEASURES SINCE THE 1990S, FUNDING THE PROTECTION OF CITY PARKS, OPEN SPACE, TRAILS, AND THE BARTON CREEK WATERSHED.

WHO ARE YOUR STRONGEST SUPPORTERS?

In 1992, conservationists in Austin, Texas, formed the Citizens for Open Space, put an open space measure on the ballot, and conducted a poll. When poll results revealed low recognition of their measure yet strong support for Save Our Springs (a higher-profile and better-financed water conservation measure), the Citizens for Open Space took notice. By partnering with the popular Save Our Springs campaign, the Citizens for Open Space communicated inexpensively and effectively through the media that saving open space and protecting watersheds went hand in hand. A vote for Citizens for Open Space was a vote for Save Our Springs. Both measures won on election day.

Local leaders in Austin understood that public awareness and the credibility of sponsors and supporters can make a huge difference in the outcome of an election. It is important to use public opinion polling to identify credible endorsers—such as a mayor, sheriff, or League of Women Voters—and communicate their support to target audiences.

Testing voter opinions about the public agency or agencies that would oversee the measure's funding is also important. The reputation of the potential agency needs to be clearly understood before moving forward.

STUDYING THE RESULTS

Even with the advice of a top-notch pollster, it is important to study the poll yourself. Cross-tabs will tell you which messages move which groups of voters; examine these data carefully and consider various trends and potential scenarios. (The margin of error of a poll reflects the pollster's confidence in the results. Keep the sample size and margin of error in mind when you're reviewing the numbers. Some subsets may be too small to accurately reflect voters' sentiment.)

These numbers can help create a road map for your measure, showing the financing mechanism and the taxing tolerance acceptable to swing voters, illustrating conservation priorities, helping to determine the appropriate election date, and many other important points. Combined with research, community outreach, and local politics, the poll numbers can help you make a judgment about every aspect of measure development and campaign management.

POLLING MATRIX

TYPE OF QUESTION
Issues/Priorities

OBJECTIVE
To put the issue of conservation in context with other community priorities

PLACEMENT IN POLL
Near the beginning

SAMPLE WORDING
Which do you think is the most serious issue facing our community? (a) growth and development, (b) education, (c) loss of open space, (d) crime, or (e) taxes and uncontrolled government spending

---

TYPE OF QUESTION
Threshold

OBJECTIVE
To determine whether a measure can win and which groups are base, swing, and opposing

PLACEMENT IN POLL
Once at the beginning and again after pro-and-con arguments are heard (test the measure as it would be worded)

SAMPLE WORDING

If the election were held today, would you be inclined to support or oppose the following measure: Shall the county issue general obligation bonds in the amount of $25 million to fund land preservation, by purchasing open land in order to alleviate traffic congestion in high-growth areas and to protect water quality, natural lands, wildlife areas, and wetlands? *Test the question again near the end of the poll in the following way:* Now that you've heard arguments for and against this measure, are you inclined to support or oppose it, or are you undecided? Is that strongly support or strongly oppose?

TYPE OF QUESTION
Spending level

OBJECTIVE
To determine the maximum spending level that voters will comfortably support

PLACEMENT IN POLL
In the middle

SAMPLE WORDING
How much in additional taxes would you be willing to pay each year to protect open space and maintain existing parks? ($5, $10, $15, none, and so on)

TYPE OF QUESTION
Financing mechanism

OBJECTIVE
To determine preferences for various types of financing mechanisms

PLACEMENT IN POLL
In the middle

SAMPLE WORDING
Costs being the same, which taxing mechanism would you most support? (a) general obligation bond, (b) sales tax, or (c) real-estate transfer tax

---

TYPE OF QUESTION
Conservation priorities

OBJECTIVE
To assess the levels of support for various conservation programs

POLLING MATRIX
(CONTINUED)

PLACEMENT IN POLL
Varies

SAMPLE WORDING
The proposed open space measure could fund a variety of conservation projects. Please tell me how important you think each of the following objectives are on a scale of 1 to 10 where 1 is not important and 10 is very important: preserving farmland, protecting important historical sites, preserving open space for outdoor recreational activities such as hiking and biking, preserving open space to stop urban sprawl, nature education for children, protecting drinking water sources, and so on.

TYPE OF QUESTION
Arguments for and against

OBJECTIVE
To assess the strength of various arguments for and against a conservation financing measure

PLACEMENT IN POLL
Varies

SAMPLE WORDING
I'm going to read you some reasons that people have given in support of public funds for open space and parkland preservation. For each one, please tell me whether you think it is a very convincing reason, a somewhat convincing reason, or not a convincing reason at all: (a) children and grandchildren deserve a future with the same beautiful landscapes that we have today, (b) if we don't save some of our open space now, it will be lost forever to new development, (c) $2.50 a month is a small price to pay to protect drinking water, parks, and wildlife, (d) our landscapes and outdoor recreational opportunities are vital to tourism, which helps our local economy, and (e) protecting open space and natural lands can play a very important role in preserving the quality of life in our area.

I'm going to read you some arguments against a proposed open space initiative. Please tell me if these statements make you more or less likely to support the measure. Is that much more or less or only somewhat more or less likely? (a) too much land will be taken off the tax rolls, resulting in an increase in property taxes, (b) we should concentrate on maintaining the land we already have instead of buying new land, (c) government cannot be trusted to spend new tax dollars wisely and effectively, and (d) there are greater priorities (schools, roads, and so on) that deserve our money and attention.

TYPE OF QUESTION
Endorsement

OBJECTIVE
To assess the strength of potential endorsing individuals and organizations

PLACEMENT IN POLL
Near the end

SAMPLE WORDING
I'm going to read you a list of people and organizations. Please tell me whether their position would make you more or less likely to support or oppose an open space conservation measure.

TYPE OF QUESTION
Demographics

OBJECTIVE
To determine voters' ages, ethnicity, income, profession, and so on

PLACEMENT IN POLL
At the end

SAMPLE WORDING
What is your age? What is your ethnicity? What is your annual income? What is your profession?

CASE STUDY: POLL RESULTS HELP SHAPE CONSERVATION ISSUE IN MASSACHUSETTS GUBERNATORIAL RACE

POLL TYPE: Nonpartisan advocacy

JURISDICTION: Commonwealth of Massachusetts

DATE: April 2002

SAMPLE SIZE: 640 registered voters

MARGIN OF ERROR: +/- 4 percent

POLLSTER: American Viewpoint and The Kitchens Group

BACKGROUND: State land conservation in Massachusetts is typically funded with periodic bonds passed by the legislature. In addition, state funding was secured for the Community Preservation Act (CPA), legislation approved in 2000 that provides matching funds to cities and towns that levy a property tax surcharge, with voter approval, to protect open space, preserve historic buildings, and create and maintain affordable housing. Still, more funding is needed to protect the state's threatened open spaces—lands identified in a statewide mapping project.

POLL OBJECTIVES: The primary objectives of the poll were to assess the level of public support for the creation of a statewide funding source dedicated to land conservation (particularly in relation to other issues) and public conservation priorities, and communicate findings to statewide political leaders. In particular, it was important to accurately frame the issue in the 2002 governor's race, informing candidates of the public's conservation priorities and helping the eventual winner develop a conservation agenda that reflects these priorities.

KEY FINDINGS:

· Land conservation in Massachusetts was an issue that just about everyone agrees on. People strongly supported the goals of a land conservation program—protecting drinking water sources, land along rivers and streams, wildlife habitat, recreation, and so on.

· Despite pessimism about the economy and the state budget deficit, an overwhelming majority of respondents felt that it was important for Massachusetts to have a program dedicated to land conservation.

· When informed about the state's rate of development, most people polled felt that current levels of state government funding for conservation were too low.

· By a 2:1 margin, voters polled said they would even be willing to pay more in taxes in order to preserve the state's remaining natural lands before they are lost to development.

SAMPLE QUESTION: "Would you be more or less likely to vote for a candidate for governor or the state legislature who supported creating a dedicated funding source for land conservation that would significantly increase funding in order to purchase and protect Massachusetts' last remaining important open space and natural lands before they are lost to development?"

Earlier questions established widespread support for state land conservation programs and funding, even in light of the recession and state budget problems. The results of this question showed that conservation is an issue that every candidate should support. In order to make the question tougher, the phrases "dedicated funding source" and "significantly increase funding" were used.

USE OF POLL RESULTS: Gubernatorial candidates were informed of the poll results.

IMPACT: The poll contributed to the successful advocacy of a state environment bond for $707 million enacted in July 2002. A representative of the conservation organization that led the polling effort was also asked to join the new governor's transition team.

CONSIDERING FOCUS GROUPS

A focus group is an in-depth qualitative interview with a small group of people that is used to probe voters' feelings and beliefs about an issue.[19] Directed by a moderator, the group discusses the issues in question, relating personal experiences and opinions in a controlled but relaxed setting. Focus groups—like polls—can be an invaluable tool for measuring public opinion. Focus groups do not offer the quantitative data of a poll, but they do help reveal the meaning behind the numbers—why people feel a certain way and the intensity and story behind those feelings.

Focus groups have several direct applications. First, they can help with the design of a poll by allowing pollsters to pretest ideas and craft the most appropriate survey questions. Focus groups also help pollsters interpret poll results, providing insights about issues otherwise unavailable. This additional information can be invaluable during the design of a conservation finance measure that truly reflects voters' attitudes and opinions. Finally, focus groups can be useful once a measure is on the ballot, helping to refine campaign messages and themes. Larger campaigns often use focus groups to test responses to television advertising before expensive airtime is purchased. Costs, however, often preclude lower-budget campaigns from taking advantage of focus groups.

Before you move forward with a focus group, keep these pointers in mind:

· Select a qualified, professional firm with experience conducting focus groups.

· Carefully consider the composition of the focus group. Just like a poll, the sample is important. If the budget allows, you will probably test selected groups of swing

PHOTO BY KEN SHERMAN

VOTERS IN OCEAN COUNTY, NEW JERSEY, THE STATE'S FASTEST-GROWING COUNTY, CREATED A NATURAL LANDS TRUST FUND IN 1997.

voters in a series of focus groups. The key is to assemble as homogeneous a group as possible—women voters or older voters, for instance. People are typically more open and honest around what they perceive to be like-minded individuals.[20] Between 6 and 12 people is an ideal size.

· Craft open-ended, neutral questions that encourage discussion and debate. The questions should be designed to gather in-depth information, yet in a way that is comfortable for participants.

· Ensure that the moderator conducts a well-organized session that promotes the free flow of ideas and opinions. Participants should fully understand the process before it begins, including the confidential nature of the results.

· Work with the focus group firm to interpret the results. Unlike a poll, the results are subjective and must be carefully assessed.

ADVANTAGES AND DISADVANTAGES
OF FOCUS GROUPS

ADVANTAGES

· A wide range of information can be gathered in a relatively short time.

· The moderator can explore related but unanticipated topics as they arise in the discussion.

· Focus groups do not require complex sampling techniques.

DISADVANTAGES

· The sample is neither randomly selected nor representative of a target population, so the results cannot be generalized or treated statistically.

· The quality of the data is influenced by the skills and motivation of the moderator.

· Focus groups lend themselves to a different kind of analysis than would be carried out with survey results. In surveys, the emphasis is on counting and measuring versus coding/classifying/sorting in a focus group.

SOURCE: Reprinted with permission from *What Are Focus Groups?* Copyright © 1997 by the American Statistical Association. All rights reserved.

In 2000, focus groups helped organizers of California's Propositions 12 and 13 find a winning solution to one of their most significant challenges—passing both measures on the same ballot. Prop 12 was the $2.1 billion Safe Neighborhood Parks, Clean Water, Clean Air and Coastal Protection Bond Act—the largest park bond in California's history.[21] Proposition 13 was a $1.97 billion water quality and flood protection bond. Both propositions included money to protect the state's water quality, watersheds, wetlands, and waterways—top priorities for the state's voters.

Focus groups indicated that voter confusion between the two measures was inevitable. Many voters also felt compelled to choose between the two. While the measures were distinct, they were also complementary, and voters in the focus groups were more inclined to support both when their messages were linked. This sentiment was not easily detected in a poll and thus proved the usefulness of focus groups for specific purposes.

Advocates of Propositions 12 and 13 joined forces to communicate the comprehensive water quality protection benefits of the measures: Proposition 12 focused on coastal land, wetlands, and watershed protection, while Proposition 13 included funds for flood control, safe drinking water, water recycling, and water supply reliability and infrastructure projects. The partnership helped the campaigns communicate a winning message for two measures at a reduced cost.

CONDUCTING A COMMUNITY ASSESSMENT

Community outreach is another useful way to solicit ideas and opinions about local greenprinting plans and conservation funding options. Done effectively, outreach brings residents to the decision-making table and helps generate public support. The approach is less costly than polling and focus groups, but it is also less scientific. As such, a community assessment should complement rather than replace these other methods.

Often a series of informal community meetings are held early in the process to solicit public opinion and help design a conservation program. Information from these meetings can help steer the program and design a measure. In particular, community insights can help shape a public poll by guiding questions and providing background about key issues.

CALIFORNIA STATE PROPOSITIONS 12 AND 13
30-SECOND TELEVISION SPOTS

SPOT #1

Propositions 12 and 13—two initiatives designed to work together to protect California's water supply.

Prop 12 protects land around lakes, rivers, and streams.

Prop 13 increases water supply, protects groundwater, and repairs aging pipes.

And both measures have safeguards built in to prevent waste.

12 and 13 will have annual independent audits to make sure the money is spent properly.

Props 12 and 13 will protect California's water and the people who drink it.

SPOT #2

Water is such a fundamental part of our lives, it's easy to forget how completely we depend on it.

Propositions 12 and 13 work together in a comprehensive program to safeguard our water.

Prop 12 protects the coast and land along our lakes, rivers, and streams to improve water quality.

Prop 13 keeps drinking water free from pollution and replaces aging water pipes.

Together, 12 and 13 will protect California's water and the people who drink it.

Paid for by the TPL Land Action Fund; Ernest Cook, president.

SOURCE: Doak, Carrier, and O'Donnell

The level of community engagement will vary from community to community, depending on its size, resources, and local politics. Some communities hold dozens of meetings with a variety of constituents and interest groups to inform the process. In St. Louis, local leaders organized the region's largest community engagement effort (more than 100 community forums) to develop the St. Louis 2004 Action Plan, which included a major land conservation component.

The St. Louis process began in 1996 with Think 2004 events. These public forums sought input from more than 10,000 residents of St. Louis and surrounding metro counties about their vision of the region. An important conservation theme emerged: people value the region's rivers and streams, among the greatest in the country, which include the confluence of the Illinois, Missouri, and Mississippi Rivers.

The infrastructure was then developed to turn the vision into reality. More than 1,200 resident "experts"—volunteers who are deeply involved in an issue—worked for several months on one of six action teams and multiple task forces. Their report of more than 100 ideas for change in the St. Louis area was then brought back to the community to elicit further ideas and suggestions. The final plan was adopted in March 1998.

From the work of the community task force on open space came the Confluence Greenway, an ambitious plan for a regional park and trails system. To fund and implement this and other projects, voters passed Proposition C, the Clean Water, Safe Parks and Community Trails measure in November 2000. This bi state, multi jurisdictional measure created two new regional park districts—one in Illinois, one in Missouri—and approved a dedicated one-tenth-cent sales tax.

St. Louis represents community outreach on an enormous scale; the process helped create a vision for the entire region as well as guide the design of an ambitious conservation funding measure. It was, according to St. Louis 2004 president Peter Sortino, an unprecedented effort that local leaders hope to continue and enhance beyond 2004.[22] In most communities, creating a vision for a local greenprinting program or a funding measure will be much more limited. But this example does offer a model for public participation that can be adopted anywhere. Keep in mind the three key elements that helped make the St. Louis process a success:

· Public involvement throughout

· Leadership from knowledgeable people in the relevant fields

· A dedicated staff to work with the public and identified leaders to maintain momentum and get results

■

CHAPTER FOUR

Designing a

Winning Measure

With the passage of a state constitutional amendment in 1996, New Mexico counties were given new authority to issue voter-approved bonds to protect open space. Diverse and fast-growing Santa Fe County was the first in line to exercise the option, passing a $12 million bond in 1998 with 71 percent of the vote. After the county quickly protected more than 2,000 acres of

PHOTO BY CHARLIE O'LEARY

FUNDING TO PROTECT THE HISTORIC SANTUARIO, OR CHAPEL, IN THE VILLAGE OF CHIMAYO, NORTH OF SANTA FE, NEW MEXICO, CAME FROM THE COUNTY'S $8 MILLION BOND MEASURE OF NOVEMBER 2000. MONEY FROM THIS MEASURE IS SPECIFICALLY EARMARKED TO PROTECT OPEN SPACE AND HISTORIC AND CULTURAL SITES.

land, voters approved an $8 million bond in 2000 and a sales tax measure in 2002.

Land conservation leaders in Santa Fe County relied on research, polling, and substantial community input to design their measures and their open space plan, which they called the Open Lands and Trails Plan for the Wildlife, Mountains, Trails and Historic Places Program. This process shaped key decisions, from the level of funding to the type of land to be protected. The plan emphasized historic and cultural sites related to the 400 years of Hispanic heritage and thousands of years of Pueblo Indian settlement in the county.

If research and polling indicate that success is possible, it is time to consider designing a conservation measure. Here are some topics to think about during this phase, all of which will be addressed in this chapter:

· How much and what types of land should be targeted?

· How will lands be selected?

· What acquisition methods should be used?

· On which ballot should the measure be placed?

· How much money should the measure attempt to raise?

· What fiscal safeguards should be included in the measure?

· How should the measure be worded?

Throughout the measure design process, let the research and poll results be your guide. And always take into account the advice of local leaders—including citizens advisory committees, elected officials, and others.

As much as possible, use the poll and local advisors to help "sell" the measure and its benefits, demonstrating how the measure reflects the public's concerns and people's willingness to pay for land preservation. The design of a measure will also depend on the maturity of a community's land conservation program. Some communities have had successful programs in place for decades; their current objective may simply be to add public funds to keep things moving. Other communities may have only recently become involved in conserving land in the face of increasing growth and development. Communities with relatively new programs may need help designing and implementing a complete greenprinting plan as well as securing public funds. TPL's report series entitled *Local Greenprinting for Growth* can help with this visioning and planning process. Several topics relevant to conservation planning are summarized in this section, namely setting preservation goals; determining acquisition methods; and targeting, identifying, and prioritizing lands.

DEFINING GOALS, IDENTIFYING LAND, AND SETTING PRIORITIES

Gallatin County, Montana, is protecting farmland from encroaching development. Santa Fe County residents are making the preservation of Native American and Hispanic cultural sites a priority. Miami-Dade County is working to deter gangs and juvenile delinquency through the creation of safe parks and the expansion of recreational opportunities. As unique as these priorities are, these communities have in common a successfully defined vision and goals that reflect their needs. Their conservation priorities are understood by all involved, from program administrators to the general public.

CASE STUDY: GALLATIN COUNTY, MONTANA, ESTABLISHES THE STATE'S FIRST PURCHASE-OF-DEVELOPMENT-RIGHTS PROGRAM

BACKGROUND: In 1997, the Gallatin County commissioners appointed a diverse citizens task force to explore ways to protect the county's dwindling open space and ranchland. The Open Space Task Force (later formalized into the Open Lands Board) studied the county's growth issues, public priorities, and regulatory and non regulatory conservation options.

Polling showed strong support for a purchase-of-development-rights program to protect the county's agricultural heritage and keep land in private hands. The preservation of ranchland makes fiscal sense as well: consider that for every property tax dollar collected on agricultural land, the county spends just 25 cents; but for every tax dollar collected on residential development, the county pays $1.45 in public services such as roads, schools, and police protection. A majority of voters polled backed open space protection with a $10 million bond.

BALLOT LANGUAGE: "Shall the Board be authorized to issue and sell general obligation bonds of the County, in the amount of up to $10 million, for the purpose of preserving open space in Gallatin County by purchasing land and conservation easements from willing landowners for the following purposes: managing growth, preserving ranches and farms, protecting wildlife areas and water quality of streams and rivers, providing parks and recreation areas and paying costs associated with the sales and issue of general obligation bonds, which bonds shall bear interest at a rate to be determined by the Board, payable semiannually during a term of not to exceed 20 years and redeemable on any interest payment date after one-half of their term, with all expenditures based on recommendations of the Open Lands Board (citizens advisory committee), after public comment, and subject to an independent audit?"

RESULT: The measure was approved in November 2000 with 59 percent of the vote. Soon after the measure passed, the governor signed into law a bill to exempt farmers and ranchers from paying any additional property tax levies that might be necessary to finance the bond. This ensured that the goal of preserving working farms and ranches in Gallatin County would not be undermined.

Your feasibility assessment is crucial in determining which types of land (farmland, recreational lands, trails, wetlands, and so on) and which conservation issues (maintaining buffers between communities, protecting water quality, and so on) are most important to voters. These broad-based goals and priorities should be reflected in the ballot language and adopting ordinance.

Public priorities should be wed to sound scientific analysis and planning policy to create a greenprinting plan. This process should be guided by the appropriate experts—biologists, urban planners, hydrologists, and so on. A variety of conservation partners at the national, state, and local levels (particularly local land trusts) can also provide technical support and help communities target land parcels and define land protection criteria. (See page 197 for a list of organizations.) An inventory of natural and cultural resources and geographic information system mapping are extremely helpful. With an understanding of what exists, key areas or even individual parcels can be specifically targeted. Knowledge of these targeted areas (the protection of an aquifer recharge area or the ecosystem of a threatened species, for example) and an estimate of the number of acres needed allow a community to clearly define its program.

Lands can be recommended for acquisition through a public nomination process and/or identified by local elected leaders, staff, and advisory boards. Nominated lands can then be prioritized in a number of different ways. Some communities rely on general guidelines, goals, or land attributes to determine whether a property is eligible for protection within the program, while others base their acquisition decisions on a specific ranking system of criteria that reflect the goals of the program. Points are awarded based on how well a property meets the criteria; priority is then given to those lands with the highest ranking. While these criteria will depend on the unique conservation goals of a community, several factors are commonly applied, as follows:

LOCATION. Is land within a targeted acquisition area? Does the property serve as an extension or linkage to protected open space or farmland?

FINANCIAL STATUS. Is there a financial incentive, such as a cost share, installment purchase, bargain sale, partial donation, conservation easement, and so on?

DEVELOPMENT PRESSURE. Is the land in imminent danger of development? Is the parcel large enough to reasonably expect it to contribute to urban sprawl?

PUBLIC SUPPORT. Does the acquisition of the parcel have widespread support? Will the property benefit more than one neighborhood or the jurisdiction at large?

The prioritization system is typically designed and implemented by local government staff and advisory boards who are charged with reviewing potential parcels and determining how well they reflect the program's goals and objectives. Acquisition or easement recommendations are then presented to the legislative body. Whatever approach you take, the process by which land is selected for protection must be fair and consistent. Designing a process for prioritizing lands and educating voters about the process can be critical to the success of your measure.

NAMING PROPERTIES

In some cases the property or properties to be protected by a measure have been identified prior to its passage. There are advantages and disadvantages to this approach. Naming popular properties or demonstrating that properties are distributed throughout the community can generate public support and motivate nearby residents. Targeting properties that provide a variety of recreational opportunities can also serve to enlist the support of different constituency groups. On the other hand, identifying parcels in advance of a measure can drive up purchase prices and complicate purchase negotiations.

Communities have won and lost with both approaches. You should determine how to proceed on a case-by-case basis, using polling and research information. In general, it is probably best not to name properties unless they are very well known and very well supported; otherwise, your message could be too narrow to attract widespread support. Instead of highlighting specific parcels, consider emphasizing the general benefits that come with land conservation, such as open space, wildlife habitat, or water quality protection.

In Arnold, Missouri, voters passed a $3.5 million sales tax referendum in 1999 that exclusively funded purchase of the Collins Tract, a 119-acre piece of property threatened by development. Public opinion polling revealed that a majority of voters (59 percent) were familiar with the property and, as one of the last undeveloped parcels, wanted it permanently protected. Voters were also particularly concerned about growth and wildlife habitat—two issues impacted by the measure and highlighted during the campaign. The Collins Tract Preservation measure was approved with 53 percent of the vote. In this case, the property's purchase price had already been established through an option agreement with the Trust for Public Land, so the success of the measure did not create any difficulties with landowner negotiations.

DETERMINING ACQUISITION METHODS

Typically, communities use a combination of acquisition methods to protect a variety of different types of land—from fee-simple acquisition to conservation easements to lease/purchase contracts. The type of acquisition methods chosen may be dictated by the specific land parcels to be protected. For instance, agricultural conservation easements are probably the best approach for protecting farms and ranchland.

Whatever the anticipated approach, carefully consider whether to emphasize this information in a land conservation campaign. Although the acquisition method is important to the program, there are advantages and disadvantages to each approach that can be difficult to communicate to voters. Too much detail can result in confusion. Once again, however, this decision depends on the community. For instance, it may be important for residents in western ranching communities to understand that easements will be purchased from willing sellers while keeping farms and ranches in private ownership and in operation.

LAND TRUST PARTNERSHIPS

Public officials and community groups benefit from the leadership and partnership of the more than 1,200 land trusts around the country. A local land trust can play many key roles in the greenprinting process:

DEFINING A CONSERVATION VISION. Land trusts can help facilitate public participation, set conservation goals, and provide technical planning support throughout the visioning process.

SECURING CONSERVATION FUNDS. Land trusts can help design a conservation finance measure and secure its passage.

ACQUIRING AND MANAGING CONSERVATION LANDS. Land trusts can help facilitate the land acquisition process, adjusting such variables as time, price, and land configurations to meet the needs of both the landowners and the acquiring agency.[23] Land trusts can also serve as land management partners.

DETERMINING THE BEST TIME
TO SEEK VOTER SUPPORT

With so many attracted to the city's quality of life, access to open space, and recreational opportunities, Boise is experiencing a population boom. This influx of new residents makes Boise the fourth fastest-growing city in the nation, per capita, with nearly 200,000 people in the city and half a million in the metropolitan region. New residential developments are consuming more than 120 acres of land in the foothills per year.

To protect the city's treasured foothills, local leaders investigated public support for a conservation finance measure in 1996. Election research showed that a low-turnout election in November 1997 would not bring out the broad cross section of voters whose support, according to the poll, was essential. Based on this information, leaders deferred a ballot measure.

But the effort to build community understanding and support for land conservation continued. Four years later, the time was right. Led by former Mayor Brent Coles, a measure was designed that attracted public support and made fiscal sense for the city. Local leaders took a community-based, grassroots approach that touched on people's personal connection to the foothills, and they created a strategically targeted campaign that made a win possible. "This was a real grassroots campaign," said Coles. "This effort wasn't run by corporate or business interests, this was people who were willing to give up their evenings and weekends to get on the phone and go out into the community and get out the vote. I've never seen anything like it."

In May 2001, 60 percent of Boise voters approved a $10 million property tax levy for the preservation of wildlife habitat and recreation lands, protection of water quality, and the prevention of mudflows in the city's scenic foothills. The measure called for review by a citizens committee, an annual independent audit, and a two-year sunset clause.

Community and conservation leaders are often eager to put park and open space measures on an upcoming election ballot, even though polls show that voters lack enthusiasm. As the Boise example illustrates, postponing a ballot measure in order to build public support for parks and open space can be the best way to ensure success.

The wait may not be long. Postponing a measure may mean simply holding off a matter of months for the most beneficial election date. Your polling and research may show, for instance, that the higher the voter turnout, the greater your chances for success. A measure on a high-turnout general election ballot will provide the greatest opportunity for participation.

Voting patterns vary from community to community. There are, however, some general guidelines to consider:[24]

- Presidential general elections (every four years in November) attract the highest number of voters, followed by presidential primary elections.

- Statewide general elections (every four years in November) and primaries also attract a high number of voters.

- County and municipal elections typically attract fewer voters.

- Special elections generally attract the fewest voters.

- Senior voters are the most consistent voting block (with the highest percentage of turnout at special elections). This group also tends to be fiscally conservative.

· Younger voters are often inconsistent voters. Their highest percentage is found in high-turnout elections. This group tends to be supportive of land conservation measures.

Keep in mind that these are only guidelines. Some activists argue, for instance, that while fiscally conservative voters tend to turn out for special elections, some high-profile conservation measures can turn out voters who specifically want to vote for open space protection.[25]

To determine the most appropriate ballot on which to place the measure, study your poll, review election statistics, and try to find out what other potential measures will be on the ballot. When too many competing spending measures are on the ballot, voters may decide to reject them all. High-profile, controversial, or complex spending measures may increase voter turnout, but they may also drag down support for a land conservation measure, sometimes even spurring the creation of opposition groups.

PHOTO COURTESY OF BOISE FOOTHILLS OPEN SPACE CAMPAIGN
BOISE VOTERS APPROVED A $10 MILLION BOND IN MAY 2001 TO PROTECT THE CITY'S SCENIC FOOTHILLS.

Here are some other considerations about timing your measure:

· Build in ample time to implement your campaign strategy.

· Take advantage when possible of the sense of urgency created by rapid land development or a specific conservation controversy.

· Keep in mind that seasonal events can affect voter attitudes. (For example, some people believe that federal income taxes are on voters' minds in April. In May and June, voters may be thinking about the outdoors and parks.)[26]

SELECTING THE FUNDING SIZE AND MECHANISM

Are voters more inclined to support borrowing money or increased sales taxes? Will they spend an additional $10 or $100 a year for conservation? Will they approve two competing spending measures on the same ballot? Your poll will help you answer these questions, showing you how much voters are willing to spend and their preferred financing mechanism.

Always let your poll numbers—not the cost of the projects—be your guide. During the early planning stages of their Safe Neighborhood Parks Act, local leaders in Miami-Dade County, Florida, conducted an exhaustive survey of municipal park and recreation agencies, historical and cultural facilities, and sports venues to determine unmet needs. The park and recreation needs alone represented more than $1 billion. Public opinion polling soon followed. The results of the survey revealed that while voters were supportive of a park, recreation, and land protection measure, the majority preferred to cap spending at

$200 million. As a result, the county and municipal park agencies prioritized their projects and pared their list to reflect voters' spending tolerance. (The measure also included a clause to assure that the receiving agencies' operating and capital budgets would not be reduced in correspondence with the bond monies they were granted—an important provision to consider.)

You may need to ask voters for a smaller amount than is needed the first time around. When the program proves itself, voters may be willing to vote for additional funding on a future ballot. Reaching the conservation goal may also take a series of measures that ask voters to provide ongoing support for a successful program. In Santa Fe County, New Mexico, voters passed three conservation finance measures in less than four years, while in Bernalillo County, New Mexico, voters approved multiple conservation measures on the same ballot—a November 2000 bond issue for open space acquisition and recreation as well as an increase in an existing property tax for open space, watershed, and historic preservation.

Whatever the funding mechanism, using locally generated dollars to attract matching funds from other jurisdictions or private sources is both popular and prudent. If matching funds are available as a result of your measure, be sure to test this issue in your poll and use it accordingly.

ESTABLISHING FISCAL SAFEGUARDS

Voters are increasingly willing to spend money to conserve the land around them. But polls have also shown that voters are wary of added government spending and want assurances that their tax dollars will be spent wisely. By including appropriate fiscal safeguards in a measure, you can help increase accountability

CASE STUDY: BEAUFORT COUNTY MEASURE
REFLECTS PUBLIC TOLERANCE
FOR SPENDING

BACKGROUND: Beaufort County, South Carolina, is home to miles of sandy beaches, open marshes, winding rivers, and live oaks draped with Spanish moss—the "Beaufort look" as some residents fondly refer to it. Its scenic beauty and temperate climate have made the county one of the fastest-growing in the nation: traffic, congestion, and loss of land are the unintended consequences.

In response, local leaders designed a conservation plan and secured a dedicated funding source. The county was well prepared before it proposed a measure, studying conservation issues (with the help of the South Carolina Coastal Conservation League), appointing a citizens board to develop acquisition criteria, and assessing public priorities and spending tolerance. This process revealed strong support for bonding against existing funds rather than raising new taxes. (The county already spent about $1.5 million annually for land conservation, through a dedicated levy.) Fiscal safeguards, such as an annual independent audit, also proved popular with voters.

BALLOT LANGUAGE: "Shall Beaufort County, South Carolina, issue general obligation bonds, not to exceed $40 million for the purpose of land preservation, by purchasing open land, development rights and conservation easements in all areas of Beaufort County, in order to alleviate traffic congestion in high-growth areas and to protect water quality, natural lands, wildlife areas, farmland, parkland, coastal areas, river and wetlands, provided that all expenditure shall be prioritized based upon an official criteria and ranking system established for the County, and subject to an annual independent audit?"

RESULT: The measure was approved with 73 percent of the vote in November 2000. Voters on Hilton Head Island—Beaufort County's largest town—also passed the island's third land conservation bond on the same ballot.

---

and ensure that funds are spent properly, while assuaging voters' concerns.

These fiscal safeguards can take a variety of forms. Annual independent financial audits, typically conducted by a public entity, can help ensure that funds are being spent appropriately. Capping administrative costs also helps guarantee that conservation funds are being spent efficiently to conserve land. A sunset clause that limits the duration of a tax is another common

FISCAL SAFEGUARDS CHECKLIST

Fiscal safeguards are popular with the public and represent good public policy. Consider including one or more of the following provisions explicitly in your conservation finance measure:

ADMINISTRATIVE COSTS. Measures can stipulate the distribution of funds, including allocations to cities, towns, and nonprofit organizations, and put a limit on administrative costs. Capping administrative costs at between 2 and 10 percent of total funds is typical.

SUNSET CLAUSE. Test in a poll whether the duration of a tax impacts the level of support. (Sample poll question: Suppose you learned that instead of lasting 20 years, the sales tax would last for 10 years . . . or 5 years. Would this make you more inclined, less inclined to support the measure, or would it make no difference?)

INDEPENDENT CITIZENS COMMITTEE. A committee can be established to oversee expenditures, design a conservation program, and make recommendations to the governing body about land acquisition.

ANNUAL INDEPENDENT AUDIT. Public audits, stipulated in a measure, can account for funds and safeguard the success of a conservation program. Audits are often a routine feature of government spending programs, but the public is usually not aware of this unless it is spelled out.

technique. And prohibiting land condemnation and establishing conflict-of-interest standards for land purchases can further help ease public concerns.

Oversight by a citizens committee can provide checks on both the disbursement of funds and the selection of properties. This formally structured body is typically appointed by elected leaders. In the case of Miami-Dade County, Florida, a hands-on committee was charged with administering bond funds approved by the Safe Neighborhood Parks measure. These individuals have been at the heart of the successful neighborhood parks process, helping to shape policy and oversee the distribution of $200 million in voter-approved bond funds. The oversight committee is also responsible for reviewing and ranking all grant applications and developing administrative rules to govern the process.

In Santa Fe County, the conservation bond measure itself called for the creation of the County Open Lands and Trails Planning and Advisory Committee (COLTPAC), an independent citizens body that received high marks for its thorough and timely efforts. COLTPAC was charged with overseeing the expenditure of bond funds and guiding the county in a program to evaluate, acquire, develop, and manage open lands and trails.

Finally, there are ways to prevent arbitrary or unnecessary changes to a land's protected status once it is acquired. In Colorado, Boulder's Open Space program prevents protected open space from being developed without an affirmative recommendation of a majority of the Open Space board of trustees and approval by the City Council.

DRAFTING BALLOT LANGUAGE

Designed to protect land and expand parks in four counties and one major city across two states, St. Louis's Proposition C broke new ground in the conservation finance arena. This historic measure, officially known as the Clean Water, Safe Parks and Community Trails Initiative, called for the creation of separate park districts in Missouri and Illinois, funded by new sales tax revenues. Voters in each jurisdiction approved the measure, which would fund the establishment of a system of interconnected parks and open space, complete with hiking and biking trails.

To establish the park districts and the taxing authority, the lead organization, St. Louis 2004, shepherded legislation through both the Missouri and Illinois legislatures. Legislation was drafted requiring that every eligible jurisdiction use the same ballot title and ballot summary. By doing so, proponents were assured that voters in each community would receive the same information about the measure—one guided by research, tested by polls, and shaped by community input. Conservation proponents in St. Louis clearly understood the importance of well-designed ballot language.

The measure's wording is the last—and sometimes the only—thing a voter will see before casting a vote. That is why advocating for the most informative and effective ballot language may be the most important thing you do. Review ballot laws and regulations to know what wording is prohibited and what is acceptable. Finally, make sure the wording of the ballot measure reflects public priorities.

Ballot measures can take a variety of forms depending on state and local election ordinances and traditions: some are simple titles and questions, some include more plain-spoken summaries, still others include pages of arguments for and against the measure. In California, for instance, designated supporters and opponents (generally public officials) can submit arguments and rebuttals; for

PHOTO BY TED CURTIS

FROM A GRASSROOTS EFFORT IN ST. LOUIS CAME AN AMBITIOUS PLAN TO CREATE AN INTERCONNECTED SERIES OF RIVERBANK PARKS FROM THE GATEWAY ARCH TO THE BLUFFS OVERLOOKING THE ILLINOIS RIVER'S CONFLUENCE WITH THE MISSISSIPPI, SOME 40 MILES NORTH.

a cost, additional arguments by others can be included in the ballot pamphlet mailed to voters. If you chose to do this, carefully select organizations and individuals to sign the arguments.

Ballot language authors also vary: in some jurisdictions, measures are written by the state attorney general or the county counsel, while in others, the local governing body (legislature, county supervisors, or city council) may write and adopt the language. In any event, you should figure out the process and how to participate in it. Your chances of success are greatest if the ballot title fairly summarizes the land conservation benefits.

Carefully study your poll before determining the most effective ballot title and wording to propose to the ballot language authors. Above all, keep the words and title simple, avoid jargon or technical language, and make sure both reflect voters' priorities. The successful Safe Neighborhood Parks Act in Los Angeles County took this approach. The term "Safe" reflected voters' concerns about crime and park safety—especially among senior citizens. "Neighborhood" let voters know that benefits would be widespread. And "Parks" was a more popular term than "open space." Proposition A's full title was the Los Angeles County Safe Neighborhood Parks, Gang Prevention, Tree-Planting, Senior and Youth Recreation, Beaches, and Wildlife Protection Act. Notes Corey Brown, one of the measure's authors, the title was accurate and inclusive, "showing nearly every voter that there was something in it for them."

QUALIFYING AN INITIATIVE

A ballot measure may be a referendum, one that is referred by the legislative body, or an initiative, one placed on the ballot by citizens' petition. If you are considering an initiative, start early. It can take months to gather the signatures necessary to qualify.

Closely review the regulations and requirements governing initiatives, including petition format, signature requirements, and filing deadlines. The sponsoring entity must be prepared to print petitions and collect signatures. There are professional signature-gathering firms that can help with the process or supplement the work of volunteers. Be prepared to gather roughly 50 percent more than the number of signatures required (which is often a percentage of voter turnout from a previous election). Invalid signatures will be thrown out. The appropriate elections office will review petitions and signatures before placing a measure on the ballot.

BALLOT MEASURE CHECKLIST

· What is the process for getting a measure on the ballot? Who is involved in that process?

· What is the deadline for referring a measure to the ballot?

· What form does the measure take? Some jurisdictions require a ballot title or number, summary, or arguments along with the ballot language. Are there word limits for each?

· Who is responsible for drafting ballot language? What is the process for approving language, title, and so on?

· Is it possible to negotiate where on the ballot the measure will be placed?

· Are mail-in ballots allowed? If so, when are they distributed, when are they due, and what is the process for collecting ballots? (See page 177 for more information about this process.)

· Can an informational mail piece that explains the measure be sent from the local government? (See page 142 for more information.)

CASE STUDY: COLORADO COMMUNITY APPROVES SALES TAX MEASURE WITH FISCAL SAFEGUARDS

BACKGROUND: Voters in Adams County, Colorado, rejected a one-fifth-cent open-space sales tax in 1997. Victory came just two years later when voters approved a sales tax measure in the same amount to prevent sprawl, and to protect natural lands, farmland, and wetlands. What changed? The winning measure included several fiscal safeguards, such as the creation of an independent citizens commission, an annual independent audit, and a sunset clause. The ballot language limited the use of the proceeds to specific conservation and recreation uses that were shown to be public priorities in a measure design poll—limiting sprawl, protecting wetlands, rivers, streams, and so on.

1997 BALLOT LANGUAGE: "Shall Adams County taxes be increased $5 million (first full-year dollar increase) by a countywide sales tax of one-fifth of one percent (one fifth of one cent per dollar) for fifteen years (terminating December 31, 2013) for the purpose of acquiring, constructing, equipping, operating, and maintaining open space and parks and recreation facilities (the Open Space Sales Tax); and shall all or a portion of the revenues from such tax be deposited into a special fund to be known as the Adams County Open Space Sales Tax Capital Improvement Fund and utilized solely to provide the capital improvements authorized in Adams County resolution No. 97-2 or for repayment of bonds; and shall all revenues from such tax and any earnings on such revenues (regardless of amount) constitute a voter-approved revenue change; and shall such tax be imposed, collected, administered and enforced as provided in Adams County resolution No. 93-1, as amended by Adams County resolution No. 97-2?"

RESULT: The measure was rejected with 39 percent of the vote.

1999 BALLOT LANGUAGE: "Shall Adams County taxes be increased $5.5 million, and whatever amounts are raised annually thereafter, by a countywide sales tax of one fifth of one percent (20 cents on a $100 purchase), effective January 1, 2000, and automatically expiring after 7 years, with the proceeds to be used solely to preserve open space in order to limit sprawl, to preserve farmland, to protect wildlife areas, wetlands, rivers, and streams, and for creating, improving, and maintaining parks and recreation facilities, in accordance with resolution 99-1, with all expenditures based on recommendations by a citizens advisory commission and subject to an independent audit?"

RESULT: The measure was approved with 60 percent of the vote.

■

CHAPTER FIVE

Running a
Conservation Campaign

Imagine that you have decided to launch a business. To turn a profit, you must sell your new product to a defined number of consumers in your community. To reach your goal, you have to develop a business plan that includes advertising and marketing strategies, find office space, staff the operation, and generate the sales. The hook: you have only a few months and an unknown amount of seed money to pull it all together. Welcome to the world of campaign management.

That said, don't panic. You'll be amazed at what can be accomplished in a short period by a dedicated, energetic group of people—particularly when it comes to protecting threatened lands.

Of course, it helps to be prepared, which is the purpose of this chapter. Included are sections on conservation campaign strategy and planning, and details from the nuts and bolts of an organization to the development of campaign themes and messages.

Keep in mind that every campaign is unique. As a result, every campaign must develop its own unique campaign strategy—a game plan that addresses the particular issues and challenges at hand. The variables are considerable: What are the voting patterns of the electorate? Who are your swing voters and how can you best reach them? What resources—financial, staff, volunteers, media—do you have at your disposal? What themes and messages are most persuasive? What environmental or land conservation issues are in the news?

As political campaign consultant S. J. Guzzetta said, "The factors and combinations are seemingly endless. Every variable factor and combination of factors creates its own nuances and subsequent responses."[27] No campaign manual—however thorough—will be able to address all the variables of your particular campaign. Be sure to understand which questions to consider, rely on your research and polling data to design a strategy, and—whenever possible—work closely with a professional campaign consultant.

It is also important to remain flexible. Campaigns are fluid and strategies evolve over time. While you must prepare, you must also be willing to adapt to changing circumstances—whether it is unexpected free press coverage, fewer fundraising dollars, attacks by opponents, or a flurry of able-bodied volunteers. Limited time and resources (financial and human) will require you to make difficult decisions. For instance, some campaigns may forgo a paid phone program or even a headquarters in order to put all of their resources into direct mail. Remember that there is no one "right" approach; any one campaign can take a variety of approaches and come out on top.

KEEPING IT LEGAL

It is essential to understand and comply with all legal requirements before any campaign activity begins. Even seemingly minor mistakes—such as incorrectly filling out forms or filing too late—can spell disaster for a campaign. The rules in some communities may be so complex that you will want to hire legal counsel, particularly to advise on financial reporting rules and requirements. This professional can help guide the campaign

CASE STUDY: CAMPAIGN HELPS LAUNCH LOCAL GREEN SPACES INITIATIVE

Former Georgia Governor Roy Barnes introduced a green space initiative in 1999, setting out an ambitious program of permanently protecting open space in the state's fastest-growing counties. To receive state funding, each eligible county had to design a strategy to protect 20 percent of its land area. In fast-growing DeKalb County just east of Atlanta, plans for the creation of a green space land acquisition program were jump-started after the governor's proposal. Once they adopted a conservation plan, the county became eligible for roughly $3 million annually in state funds.

DeKalb County leaders knew that significant local funds were also essential to fully implement their plan. As a newly elected county CEO, Vernon Jones became a forceful champion of the green space program, immediately referring a $125 million general obligation bond to the upcoming March 2001 special election ballot after taking office that January. By doing so, he saved money on another election later on and took advantage of the momentum building about the issue.

Still, this left just two months to raise money and organize a campaign. The campaign leaders were clearly up to the task. An effective grassroots effort

PHOTO BY BUD SMITH

I DON'T KNOW A SINGLE POLITICIAN WHO CAN LOSE BY CAMPAIGNING ON THE ISSUE OF PARKS AND SAVING GREEN SPACE AND PRESERVING WATER QUALITY. THIS ISSUE CUTS ACROSS ALL POLITICAL LINES. IT IS NOT BOUND BY RACE OR BY PARTISAN POLITICS OR BY AGE.

VERNON JONES, CHIEF EXECUTIVE OFFICER
DEKALB COUNTY, GEORGIA

was implemented, with outreach to neighborhoods, community groups, business leaders, churches, and other public forums. Direct mail, radio, cable television, a web site, and signs also helped inform voters about the measure's benefits.

Voters approved the measure with an overwhelming 70 percent margin, attracting support from all parts of the county.

through the critical and sometimes confusing legal issues involved in running a campaign. If the costs of outside counsel are beyond your budget, name an election law attorney to your advisory committee or find another pro bono legal source.

Legal requirements cover a wide range of campaign-related issues that are governed by federal, state, and local jurisdictions. These legal requirements are categorized as follows:

STATE AND LOCAL CAMPAIGN FINANCE LAWS.
These laws set limits on raising, spending, and reporting campaign contributions.

FEDERAL, STATE, AND LOCAL ELECTION LAWS.
State and local election laws that are not related to finance include such topics as disclaimers on campaign materials, posting requirements for campaign signs, rules regarding election day activities, and so on.

POSTAL REQUIREMENTS. The U.S. Post Office has specific requirements for sending political mail using bulk rate and nonprofit postal permits.

INTERNAL REVENUE SERVICE (IRS) LOBBYING LAWS. Nonprofit public charities that try to influence legislation—including ballot measures—are deemed to be lobbying by the IRS. These organizations are subject to expenditure limits and IRS reporting requirements.

Keep in mind that laws and regulations governing campaigns and elections vary from state to state and community to community. Even within a jurisdiction, the rules are often in flux. That is why it is important to review the election laws in your community and check regularly throughout the campaign to find out if changes have been made. The state governing body (the secretary of state, ethics commission, public disclosure commission, or equivalent) and your local elections office can provide you with the rules and regulations.

STATE AND LOCAL CAMPAIGN FINANCE LAWS

Several steps need to be taken before a campaign can raise and spend money legally. These include the formation of a campaign committee, appointment of a treasurer, and the establishment of a bank account. It is also essential to have an understanding of contribution and expenditure limits and financial reporting requirements.

A formally established campaign committee is a legal entity registered with the appropriate governing jurisdiction. Officers must be named and the committee will probably receive an identification number. A campaign *advisory* committee, on the other hand, is not a legal entity; its size, structure, and even its existence are up to each campaign.

Check with the secretary of state or local elections office to obtain a registration form and instructions for establishing your committee. Individuals who serve as chair, vice-chair, secretary, and treasurer can be called upon to provide general guidance to the campaign and carry out key tasks. Determine the responsibilities of each position based on the legal requirements and the needs of your campaign. For instance, the treasurer is a key position that entails significant work and responsibility. Your chair may provide direction to the entire campaign and advisory committee. If the campaign is very small, however, you may need this person in name only.

When you select the name for your committee, remember your message (the Committee for Safe Parks, the Committee for Clean Water, and so on); the committee name will be on your letterhead and on every piece of advertising you distribute. And check out any legal restrictions. Some jurisdictions have laws about what you can and cannot name your committee.

Before you raise a penny, the campaign should also determine how to report contributions and expenditures, and any other finance reporting regulations. Your campaign treasurer is responsible for tracking contributions and expenditures and filing necessary reports. Make sure the rules are followed exactly. Even minor financial reporting oversights have the potential of tarnishing your campaign's image and weakening support.

Some pointers: Don't rely on what you or someone you know has done in the past; regulations tend to change frequently. Don't rely on this or any other campaign handbook; the limits and reporting requirements will vary from state to state and even community to community. Go straight to the source: the secretary of state and your local elections department. These offices will provide you with the information you need to raise and spend money legally. Here are some key questions to ask:

· What information must accompany a contribution (name, address, contribution amount, check date, copy of check, and so on)?

· What reports are required and to which agency? State and local filing may be required. And remember that if the committee's gross receipts are expected to exceed $25,000, you must file a Form 990 tax information return with the IRS.

· What format should be followed for making financial reports, whose signatures are required, and when are they due? Is electronic filing possible or required?

· What are the rules for in-kind contributions (donations of office space, equipment, and so on) and how must they be reported?

· What are limitations and requirements for accepting loans to the campaign?

· How should expenditures be itemized?

FEDERAL, STATE, AND LOCAL ELECTION LAWS

There are myriad laws and regulations guiding campaign activities that do not involve raising and spending money. For instance, some communities have strict regulations about where and when you can post campaign signs. Others have specific disclaimer requirements for direct mail and paid, recorded telephone calls. At the federal level, campaign literature cannot be placed in or around mailboxes, which are considered federal property. And publicly owned buildings may not be used for campaign purposes.[28] Once again, check the rules and regulations before you act.

Disclaimer rules deserve particular attention. Disclaimers are used to identify the source of campaign material with such information as committee name, address, and officers. Disclaimers are typically required for a campaign's printed materials (stationery, checks, and other legal documents) and paid advertising (direct mail, radio, and television). Find out exactly what information needs to be included, such as specific wording and size requirements and whether the committee identification number is required. If you don't have a campaign headquarters, open up a post office box or use the address of one of the campaign officers or staff.

A disclaimer for advertising may read as follows:

"Paid for by the Committee for Clean Water and Open Space"
123 Main Street
Burlington, Vermont 05401

Jane Smith, Chairman
Bob Jones, Treasurer
Campaign ID number 654321

Several legal issues involving staff and liability should be considered during the early stages of a campaign. If your campaign is hiring staff, you should obtain a Federal Employer Identification Number (FEIN), sometimes known as a Taxpayer Identification Number (TIN). The FEIN helps establish the committee as a separate legal entity for tax purposes. You will also need a FEIN to open a bank account for the committee and for all other IRS reporting. (If the campaign is sponsored by an incorporated group, such as The Conservation Campaign, the group's number would be used.) In addition, you must determine whether workers are employees or independent contractors. This decision determines what benefits and legal protections the worker is entitled to, and whether payroll taxes must be withheld and paid on that worker's compensation.

Finally, the committee should consider obtaining insurance. This can be done fairly easily: insurance carriers will typically provide up to $5 million for approximately $500.

POSTAL REQUIREMENTS

The only cost-effective way to send campaign literature to large numbers of voters is by bulk rate. Rules and regulations for distribution of political bulk mail are governed by the U.S. Post Office. Any organization, for-profit or nonprofit, may purchase a bulk mail permit. This permit allows for mass mailings at discounted rates. Additional nonprofit discounts are given only to qualified organizations that apply for the right.

To send political bulk mail, you need to apply for a permit or obtain permission to use a bulk mail vendor's permit. You must also understand the size and wording requirements for a legal bulk mail indicia and file with the post office for each mailing. (See page 146 for a description of this process.)

Organizations with nonprofit status may also obtain nonprofit postal permits and benefit from postal rates that are even further discounted. This is true for both nonprofit public charities recognized under section 501(c)(3) of the Internal Revenue Code and nonprofit social welfare organizations recognized under section 501(c)(4). The postage savings are about six cents per piece of mail. For a campaign that relies heavily on direct mail, the savings in postage may amount to several thousand dollars.

However, a nonprofit corporation must never "lend" its nonprofit mailing permit to a campaign. To do so will place the organization's nonprofit rate in serious jeopardy. It is perfectly legal for a nonprofit to mail literature that advocates a yes or no vote on a ballot measure, but the nonprofit must devise, design, and pay for the literature. This is a strict legal test and may safely be pursued only with the advice of specialized counsel.

IRS LOBBYING LAWS

Public charities may participate in ballot measure campaign activities in a number of ways, but they are subject to special Internal Revenue Service expenditure limits and reporting requirements. The fundamental principle to know is that the IRS considers any effort by a public charity to influence the outcome of a ballot measure to be lobbying. Most charities that lobby or that plan to lobby choose to be governed by section 501(h) of the Internal Revenue Code. This section establishes a formula that determines how much a charity may safely spend on all lobbying activities—direct and grass roots. All activity on a ballot measure, including expenses in support of placing a petition or an initiative on the ballot, is considered direct lobbying and therefore subject to the more generous expenditure limits than grassroots lobbying. Direct lobbying can include drafting ballot measures, developing strategies to place measures on the ballot, public opinion polling, and any express advocacy for or against a measure, such as direct mail, newspaper ads, or grassroots canvassing.[29]

The following chart sets forth the limits for total lobbying and total grassroots lobbying expenses, which are correlated to an organization's total exempt purpose expenditure budget. All lobbying expenses must be reported annually to the Internal Revenue Service on the exempt organization's tax return.

EXEMPT PURPOSE EXPENDITURES	TOTAL LOBBYING LIMIT (DIRECT PLUS GRASSROOTS)	TOTAL GRASSROOTS LOBBYING LIMIT
Up to $500,000	20 percent (up to $100,000)	5 percent (up to $25,000)
$500,000 to $1 million	$100,000 + 15 percent of excess over $500,000	$25,000 + 3.75 percent of excess over $500,000
$1 million to $1.5 million	$175,000 + 10 percent of excess over $1 million	$43,750 + 2.5 percent of excess over $1 million
$1.5 million to $17 million	$225,000 + 5 percent of excess over $1.5 million	$56,250 + 1.25 percent of excess over $1.5 million
$17 million and over	$1 million	$250,000

SOURCE: *Foundations and Ballot Measure: A Legal Guide*, Thomas R. Asher (Washington, D.C.: The Alliance for Justice, 1998).

So what kind of expenses might a public charity appropriately incur that need to be tracked and reported to the IRS?

· Cash contributions to a ballot measure committee or any other entity that is raising funds to get a measure on the ballot or to influence the outcome of a ballot measure

· All expenses related to raising funds for a campaign, including raising contributions to your own organization as well as contributions to another entity, such as a campaign committee

· The costs of any communications you make to voters reflecting an opinion on the measure

· All personnel costs that may reasonably be attributed to the campaign, along with an allocation of indirect costs

Here, in summary, are the IRS rules for 501(c)(3) public charities that participate in ballot measure campaigns:

- Never allow any funds, facilities, or staff and volunteers of your organization, or who may appear to represent your organization, to be used or act in any way to support or oppose a candidate for public office, or to be connected with the activity of any political party.

- Seek legal advice to find out whether you should elect 501(h) or be governed by the complex rules that apply to nonelecting charities. If your organization has elected to be governed by IRS section 501(h), calculate your lobbying ceiling and make sure your campaign activities won't take you over the top.

- Carefully keep track of all expenditures on ballot measure campaigns, including campaign contributions, in-kind expenditures (don't forget staff time), and costs related to placing the initiative on the ballot.

- Report all ballot measure expenditures to the IRS on Form 990 as direct lobbying. (In addition, most states will require at least some of these expenditures be reported on state forms.)

- If you solicit contributions to your organization for a ballot measure campaign, you must advise potential donors that their contributions are not tax deductible. Also, never solicit or accept funds from a private foundation for a campaign. Finally, if you are raising funds, almost every state will require you to register a campaign committee and to comply with state campaign finance laws regarding reporting contributions and expenditures.

CORPORATE CAMPAIGN COMMITTEES

Most campaign committees are considered to be "independent." They are a temporary association of people who join together briefly to influence a ballot measure election and disband after the election. But corporations may also register campaign committees. In that case, the campaign committee shares some attributes of the corporation's legal and tax status. For conservation finance measures, the "parent" corporation will usually be a nonprofit conservation organization with 501(c)(3) or 501(c)(4) tax status. A corporate-sponsored campaign has several advantages over an independent campaign.

- Officers of independent committees are personally liable for the actions of the campaign, while corporations typically have a corporate liability insurance policy.

- Independent committees are technically required to file federal tax returns (though few of them do and they rarely get into trouble for failure to comply). The financial activities of a corporate committee require no separate filing because they are subsumed within the corporation's tax return.

- Nonprofit corporations typically have postal permits that grant them favorable rates, which can save lots of precious money if direct mail is a campaign strategy.

- Nonprofit organizations and corporations that specialize in conservation finance measures have expertise in conservation finance and related legal issues that can be invaluable to a local community.

Public charities that register a campaign committee must be especially careful. Remember that these organizations must take into account that all funds raised and spent by the committee will count against the organization's lobbying ceiling. A campaign that succeeds too well could blow the roof off! The charity must also make special efforts to ensure that everyone who raises money for the committee advises donors that their contributions are not tax deductible.

COMMON LEGAL MISTAKES

Complex election, postal service, and IRS laws can trip up even experienced campaigners. Here are some common legal mistakes:

- Failing to file a tax return
- Improperly reporting campaign contributions
- Missing reporting deadlines
- Using government property for campaign purposes
- Posting campaign signs incorrectly against local ordinance
- Incorrectly using bulk rate indicia (a potentially costly mistake!)
- Failing to include a disclaimer on printed materials

To avoid mistakes, check with the governing jurisdictions and legal experts for up-to-date rules and regulations.

ORGANIZING YOUR CAMPAIGN

To get your campaign started, you'll need to line up the right people, from campaign advisors to staff to volunteers. This section discusses the basic organization and infrastructure of a campaign.

CAMPAIGN ADVISORY COMMITTEE

One of the first, most important steps you'll take is to form a broad-based citizens committee to help with strategy,

THE TRUST FOR PUBLIC LAND CREATES
THE CONSERVATION CAMPAIGN, EXPANDING
CAMPAIGN SERVICES

Nonprofit 501(c)(3) organizations, like TPL, are limited in the amount they may spend on lobbying in support of legislative and ballot measures. This limitation applies to measures at the federal, state, and local levels of government. In order to promote ballot measures beyond its ceiling, TPL formed a 501(c)(4) organization in 2000 called The Conservation Campaign (TCC). This organization is a separate nonprofit corporation that may lobby without limit; its primary mission is to mobilize public support for measures that provide public financing for conservation, through bond issues, legislation, referenda, and other means. Unlike a 501(c)(3), however, contributions are not tax deductible; this entity may not receive government funding or private foundation support.

Both TPL and TCC work to increase public funding for land conservation. Their roles are usually distinct, yet at times overlap. TPL generally helps governments research and design ballot measures, activities that are not considered lobbying. Both TPL and TCC support local ballot measure campaigns with strategic advice, polling, and campaign activities—endeavors that are generally classified as lobbying. TCC handles direct campaign and lobbying activities such as forming a campaign committee, creating a campaign plan, and so on. TCC has expertise in all areas of campaign management, including compliance with campaign finance laws, and has large-volume relationships with vendors that can save money.

TCC has formed and operated many corporate campaign committees that have resulted in successful ballot measures. Examples include a $20 million land conservation bond in Dakota County, Minnesota (November 2002); an $192 million open space trust fund property tax in Morris County, New Jersey (November 2001); the creation of regional park districts in Missouri and Illinois to fund the Confluence Greenway (November 2000); and a sales tax levy in Coconino County, Arizona (November 2002) to protect natural areas and wetlands and create new county parks.

fundraising, and endorsements. A campaign advisory committee is an informal body of local leaders established to guide the campaign and lend it credibility and resources. Some of these members will likely serve as officers of your formally registered campaign committee, such as chair, secretary, or treasurer. The number of people on an advisory committee can vary; what is important is to attract a diverse group of experienced, motivated community leaders.

Seek out people who are well intentioned, politically astute, and connected to their community. That could mean a business leader who can raise campaign funds, an influential parks advocate who can speak persuasively to the issues, or a community activist who can organize a neighborhood. Most committee members should be expected to do some heavy lifting—raising funds, organizing events, chairing sub-committees, and so on. Some high-profile members, however, may simply lend prestige and credibility to the campaign, providing little hands-on assistance.

Advisory committee members will be the eyes and ears of the campaign, helping to make course corrections that reflect public priorities and communicate the benefits of the measure to the public. Time commitments will vary; two to ten hours a week is a ballpark. Committees also range in size, although ten to twelve is a workable number.

PHOTO BY DOUGLAS PEEBLES

VOTERS IN MAUI COUNTY, HAWAII, APPROVED A MEASURE TO PROTECT OPEN SPACE, NATURAL RESOURCES, AND SCENIC VIEWS IN NOVEMBER 2002. THE FIRST OF ITS KIND IN THE STATE, THE MEASURE SETS ASIDE 1 PERCENT OF EXISTING PROPERTY TAX REVENUES FOR CONSERVATION.

CAMPAIGN COMMITTEE

This is a legal entity that is registered with the governing jurisdiction. The campaign committee raises and spends campaign funds and regularly reports on its contributors and expenditures. The officers appointed to the formal committee will depend on the requirements of the jurisdiction, but typically include the campaign chair, secretary, and treasurer.

STAFF AND VOLUNTEERS

Depending on the resources available, your campaign could be run by a seasoned campaign manager or by a group of volunteers. Quite likely you'll have a mix of the two, as well as a media consultant and a pollster. Here are a couple of things to consider before staffing your campaign:

BE REALISTIC. Build your organization according to the needs of your campaign and the resources available. You may find you can get the job done without any paid staff, or you may want to invest in a professional campaign manager who can lead the effort.

BE RESOURCEFUL. Don't pay for things that you can get for free (but make sure any donations are reported appropriately).

BE PREPARED. Assess your campaign, evaluate your staff needs, and assign tasks as early as possible.

A review of common campaign roles follows. Keep in mind that for smaller campaigns, a person will likely wear more than one hat. With limited financial resources, hardworking volunteers can also fill these spots.

CAMPAIGN MANAGER. This is the person in charge of managing the operation and guiding the development of the campaign plan. The campaign manager oversees the campaign staff or volunteers and works with the pollster, consultant, campaign committee, and advisory committee to keep the campaign on track. Depending on the needs of the campaign, this individual can take on other roles as well. *Qualifications:* Strong management skills; politically astute; experience managing winning campaigns (preferably land conservation); knowledge of the community; solid relationship with key political figures in the community; an understanding of and preferably firsthand experience with each major campaign function (field operations, fundraising, and so on).

IMAGE FROM A CONSERVATION MEASURE DIRECT MAIL CAMPAIGN GETTING VOTERS TO THE POLLS ON ELECTION DAY IS THE CULMINATION OF MONTHS OF CAMPAIGN EFFORTS.

FUNDRAISING AND FINANCE COORDINATOR.
It takes a lot of people to raise a lot of money. One
person, the finance coordinator, will manage the process.
The job: to organize a finance committee, develop a
fundraising strategy, solicit donors, and oversee fundraising
events. *Qualifications:* Strong interpersonal skills; experience
raising money; an understanding of potential donors in
your campaign; knowledge of campaign finance rules
and regulations.

TREASURER. The campaign treasurer oversees expenditures and files financial reports. This person is responsible
for paying the campaign's bills and depositing and tracking
contributions. *Qualifications:* Accounting/bookkeeping
experience; knowledge of state and local reporting
requirements; organizational skills.

PRESS SECRETARY. The press secretary develops a press
plan, communicates the campaign message through the free
media, and serves as the point of contact for reporters.
(See page 161 for more on the roles of the press secretary.)
Qualifications: Good communication skills; experience working
with the press; an understanding of the media market.

FIELD COORDINATOR. This individual coordinates
direct voter contact efforts, at the door, on the phone,
and at neighborhood coffees or meetings. The job's tasks
include design of a field program and management of
volunteers and/or paid field staff. *Qualifications:* Field experience; strong organizational and management skills.

VOLUNTEER COORDINATOR. The volunteer coordinator must keep people busy, motivated, and on-track. He
or she must also keep them coming back. It is a crucial role

and in some smaller campaigns it is the most important role. *Qualifications:* Strong interpersonal, organizational, and management skills; an ability to motivate people.

It is important in any organization for people to understand their role and the roles of others. This is especially true of campaigns, where things move quickly and some positions are filled by paid staff, others by volunteers. Make sure to clearly define people's roles and keep everyone informed as your organization grows. Finally, you may need to hire campaign professionals such as a media consultant. (See page 157 for a discussion of the roles of consultants.)

CAMPAIGN HEADQUARTERS AND EQUIPMENT

Most small campaigns can manage effectively without a headquarters. In fact, the overhead costs may drain valuable resources from direct voter contact. If you do need a campaign headquarters, try to find one that is centrally located in a safe area, accessible from the street, and inexpensive or free. Pay as little as possible for a vacant storefront. Try to get office space, furniture, and equipment donated from a friendly business or supporter. (Once again, make sure any donations are appropriately reported.)

Depending on its size and location, you can use your office to house staff and volunteers, hold campaign rallies, and increase visibility. Good campaign headquarters provide ample office space for staff, storage space for supplies, and a large meeting room for volunteers. The furniture and equipment will depend on the size of your campaign. Essential furniture includes desks, tables, chairs, file cabinets, and partitions (if the office configuration is not suitable). Essential equipment includes computer software and hardware, printer, fax machine, and phones.

DESIGNING A WINNING CAMPAIGN STRATEGY

Election year 2000 was a busy one for land conservation: voters approved measures generating nearly $7.5 billion for parks and open space.[30] Among them was Santa Fe County, where radio ads were designed to raise voter awareness about a preservation bond listed at the end of a long presidential-year ballot. Across the country in Broward County, Florida, land conservation proponents used cable television and high-impact direct mail to inform voters of the link between clean water and open space protection. While these campaigns employed different techniques, each had in common a well-designed and well-executed strategy—and a successful result.

Designing a strategy is probably the most difficult yet most essential part of the campaign. But, at this point, with thorough research and polling and a well-designed measure, your foundation is solid. Take the time to develop your strategy and to make sure that all the key individuals and groups involved know how to follow it.

To get started, think about the most effective ways to communicate the most persuasive messages the greatest number of times to your targeted group(s) of voters. That may mean emphasizing water quality protection to swing voters through direct mail and walking door to door. Or it may mean increasing turnout among likely supporters with a get-out-the-vote message about a measure's recreational benefits. Most likely it will mean communicating a couple of key messages through different channels and to different targeted audiences.

Once you've made the determinations about messages and audiences, target all of your activities—from speakers bureau to free media—to reinforce your strategy. Describe these activities specifically in a campaign plan, complete with staff/volunteer assignments, budget, and timing. Throughout the process you'll be required to make tough choices about where to spend limited financial and human resources. Remember to rely on what you've learned from your research and polling, remain flexible, and consider the advice of campaign professionals whenever possible.

MESSAGE AND THEME

Women voters in Broward County, Florida, received an unusual piece of political mail in the fall of 2000. The brochure showed a photo of a young child swimming in a pool, with a caption that read, "Safe Water?" As explained in the piece, drowning is the number-one killer of children under age five in South Florida. In fact, an average of thirteen preschool-age children drown in Broward County annually. The message of the brochure: Do something about the problem by passing the Safe Parks and Land Preservation Bond Referendum in November 2000.

SOURCE: STEARNS CONSULTING, INC.

THIS DIRECT MAIL PIECE COMMUNICATES TO SWING VOTERS THE WATER SAFETY COMPONENTS OF A CONSERVATION MEASURE IN BROWARD COUNTY, FLORIDA, IN NOVEMBER 2000.

Polling showed that water safety was a key concern of women voters—an important swing voting group. The campaign talked about the water safety component of the measure to this group in an interesting and compelling way. While the measure had many land and water conservation benefits, one component called for the construction of safer, more modern swimming pools and swimming instruction for 55,000 preschool-age children.

The water safety piece conveyed one of the campaign's messages to one group of targeted voters; messages about park safety, clean water, and open space were highlighted in other paid media to other targeted groups.

The theme of a campaign defines, in a clear, succinct, and compelling way, the most popular benefits of a measure. It encapsulates the overriding purpose of the measure in such a way that its various components can always be explained within the context of the theme. For example, clean water may be the number-one priority of residents in your community. Develop a theme and messages that underscore the water quality protection benefits inherent in your land preservation measure—the preservation of watershed lands, the creation of greenways along rivers, and stream buffers to help control runoff from development. Develop a theme and title that explain the connection between open space preservation and water quality protection (for example, Measure A: Preserving Our Land, Protecting Our Water).

In addition to the overall theme of a campaign, define which specific messages move which voting groups. Preventing sprawl and traffic congestion, improving youth recreational opportunities and reducing juvenile delinquency, spending new tax dollars wisely—these are examples of some specific messages that can be communicated to various audiences. Your messages should complement your theme, provide more specific information about your measure, and be compelling. These messages should also be designed to counteract anticipated opposition. For instance, TPL has used headlines in direct mail pieces to assure tax-weary voters that new conservation funds will cost little, such as one entitled "A Dime a Day to Protect Our Heritage."

Developing a set of talking points can be an effective way to keep the campaign staff and volunteers "on message." These talking points succinctly outline the key message(s) that the campaign is trying to send and should be shared with spokespeople, surrogate speakers, key supporters, and anyone else who speaks to the public on behalf of the campaign.

IDENTIFYING BASE AND SWING VOTERS

Polling data and election statistics can help you determine the different degrees of support and opposition among voters: strong support; weak support; undecided; weak opposition; strong opposition. Strong supporters—voters who back your measure throughout the poll and are unmoved by negative arguments—are your base voters. This group does not generally need to receive persuasion messages. But don't ignore this group just because they're on your side. Some base voters may also be infrequent voters who need to be included in a get-out-the-vote effort.

The group in the middle—soft supporters and soft opponents—are your swing voters. These voters are presumed to be more persuadable and may move from one column to another after hearing pro-and-con arguments. Take a look at how voters shift position in the poll from the threshold to the follow-up questions. These swing voters can be convinced to support your measure after receiving information about it.

Swing voters are not a monolithic group; most likely you'll have several different categories of voters who respond to several different arguments. For instance, tax-sensitive senior citizens may respond well after hearing about the fiscal safeguards in the measure. Republican women voters may be on the fence until they learn about a measure's youth recreational programs. Target these groups and communicate key messages, and they may move to your column instead of your opponents'.

Finally, there is a group of voters who are strongly opposed to your measure. Your poll has told you they are unmoved by the arguments, so don't waste limited resources trying to persuade them. Do, however, respond to their public attacks—in letters to the editor, community forums, direct mail, and other communications—while refocusing attention on your message.

As mentioned earlier, it is important to identify messages and themes that tend to move swing voters away from your measure. Try to assess the strength of the opposition and how these messages will be communicated. Be prepared with responses: link up key spokespeople or organizations to rebut specific attacks. For instance, if opponents charge that a new tax will hurt the local economy, line up endorsers such as the chamber of commerce to discuss how land conservation makes good economic and business sense. Ideally, you should try to preempt the opposition with your own information about the benefits and safeguards of the measure.

TARGETING ANALYSIS: COUNTING THE VOTES

Long before any votes are counted—or even cast—you should estimate the votes you need to win. This targeting analysis is critical in a couple of cases. First, if you don't have the money to conduct a public opinion poll, a targeting analysis will help you allocate your resources more effectively. You won't know which specific demographic groups make up your base and swing voting groups, but you will know which geographic areas are most inclined to support environmental and/or spending measures and which are typically on the fence.

Next, a targeting analysis can be helpful even if you do have the benefit of a poll to help target your campaign. For instance, some states such as Georgia and Washington don't provide voter information by party, so without analysis you won't be able to target your media accordingly (although the poll will give you other demographic factors such as gender and age to consider). You may also want to refine your targeting beyond the information provided in a poll. For instance, a targeting analysis may tell you that voters in a cluster of southwestern precincts are most inclined to support environmental measures. This area may be the best place to attract supporters to a campaign kickoff or rally or to increase turnout among supporters in a low-turnout election.

Begin your targeting analysis by gathering election turnout figures from previous elections. These elections must be the same type, meaning that if your measure is on a March 2001 ballot, you should obtain statistics from the last four March elections in odd years; if your measure is being held during a presidential general election, look at turnout from recent November presidential elections.

For a more exact estimate of voter turnout for your conservation measure, look beyond the turnout for the top race (president, mayor, and so on) and determine what, if any, voter drop-off occurred for measures farther down the ballot. For instance, 50 percent of registered voters may have cast a ballot for governor while only 45 percent took the time to vote for a statewide parks bond on the same ballot.

Estimate voter turnout for your measure based on figures from the last four elections of the same type (that is, special, primary, or general). Keep in mind that there may be blips—a higher-than-normal turnout when a controversial issue or hot candidate was on the ballot. The average turnout from these past elections applied to the current number of registered voters will give you a good idea of the likely voter turnout—and the number of votes cast on your issue—this time around. Take half, two-thirds, or whatever vote is required for passage, add one, and you have the total number of votes needed to win. (Voter registration and turnout figures from previous years can be obtained from your local or state elections office, such as city clerk, county registrar of voters, or secretary of state.)

After you have determined the number of votes needed to win, you need to determine how to reach that number, precinct by precinct. The goal is to determine where you can most efficiently secure your votes. Sometimes polling shows that support from base voters is enough to win. In this case, a strong get-out-the-vote effort is all that is needed. In most cases, however, support from swing voters is needed as well. To get it, you must determine the swing precincts—those precincts that contain voters who are likely to be undecided or persuadable either way—and focus your resources accordingly. This is done by looking closely at your election research and determining which precincts were evenly divided in past fiscal and environmental measures. For instance, say that in the last five years there were ten fiscal and/or environmental measures in your city. These measures included a statewide park bond referendum, a countywide road bond, a local land conservation measure, and various city sales tax increases. Break out the vote, precinct by precinct, and perhaps you find that a third of the precincts voted consistently in favor of the spending/environmental measures. The voters in these precincts are your base voters. Another third of the precincts largely rejected the measures. Don't expect to win here. The final third of the precincts is fairly divided on the measures. These are your swing precincts—the places to target your financial and field resources.

Next, put a number beside each precinct. This is the number of voters you hope, with work, to win. For instance, based on turnout research, say you expect 40 percent of registered voters to participate in the upcoming election. With 1,000 registered voters in precinct 5, you can expect roughly 400 people to cast their ballots for or against your measure. Research also tells you that 65 percent of the voters in precinct 5 supported past fiscal and environmental measures. Sixty-five percent of 400 voters indicates an estimated 260 votes in favor of your measure—a solid, base precinct. Other precincts will clearly be in the loss-and-swing columns. Put a number by each and focus your resources on the swing precincts—those at close to 50 percent. Add up the numbers—increasing where you think you can safely expand the margin—to the specific number of voters you think you can win. (See page 172 for more information about targeting precincts and assigning volunteers.)

DEVELOPING A CAMPAIGN PLAN AND BUDGET

The campaign strategy outlines the themes and messages you are going to communicate to targeted voters: what you are going to say and to whom. The campaign plan lays out how you are going to implement your strategy and allocate your resources. It is a way to outline, in writing, all the details critical to a campaign, from the kickoff rally to phone banks to fundraising events.

A plan can take a variety of forms. It is helpful to begin with an assessment of the race that includes a profile of the jurisdiction, an overview of the key messages and targeted audiences, and any information about potential opposition and/or measures that may compete for voters' support or attention. Next comes a discussion of the most effective campaign activities or approaches. This includes a description of the activity, the anticipated costs, staff and volunteer needs, and the timing.

By putting your ideas in writing, you'll be forced to make a lot of decisions and think through how each activity is interrelated. For instance, your strategy may be to increase voter turnout among likely supporters. You decide to identify supporters from this pool over the phone. Many questions need to be answered: How many supporters are you trying to identify? Will you conduct a volunteer phone bank or hire professional phoners? Should you begin phoning before you've dropped your first piece of mail or after? Once you've identified supporters, what's your plan to get-out-the-vote?

This level of detail is needed for every aspect of the campaign, from free and paid media to field organizing. Alternatively, you can develop individual plans for such things as grassroots outreach, free media, paid media, and fundraising. Those plans can include the details that are described more generally in an overall campaign plan. Whatever the approach, describe each activity in the plan, put it down on a calendar, include it in your budget, and assign someone to implement it.

It is important to note that any plan that outlines the campaign strategy, calendar, and budget should be carefully guarded. You'll want to share information with advisory board members and other key players, but consider distributing copies to be read immediately and then returned. You may decide to create a condensed version— with fewer details—to be used as a fundraising tool. This can be a helpful way to reassure potential contributors (investors, really) that a winning strategy and plan have been developed.

TIMING YOUR CAMPAIGN ACTIVITIES

Every campaign activity should be scheduled. Include on a calendar the date of the activity as well as all the deadlines to be met during the preparation. For instance, if you're planning to drop a piece of mail the week before election day, determine the deadlines for each part of the process: concept, copy, design, proofs, printing, labels, and mailing. Build in plenty of time for unanticipated delays; there will usually be at least one for any given activity.

BUDGETING YOUR RESOURCES

Figure out your campaign strategy and what it takes to win. Put every campaign activity down in a plan. Estimate the costs of implementing this plan—from office overhead to advertising—in a budget. Then determine whether and how you can raise the money.

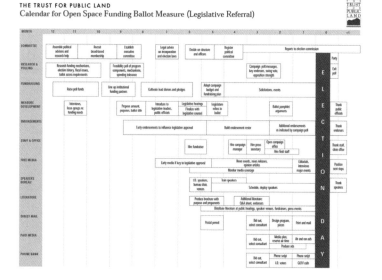

SOURCE: THE TRUST FOR PUBLIC LAND

You should consider designing a couple of budgets based on different fundraising projections. A bare-bones budget should include all fixed costs and priority campaign activities; if money flows well, a second budget can include additional activities. This process will help you define your priorities. Typically, things like campaign headquarters and equipment are considered essential budget items. This is not necessarily the case, however, with local land conservation campaigns. Depending on the circumstances, your limited budget may be better spent on direct mail or telephone banks. The point is to put all your goals down in writing and then make priorities.

Be as specific as possible in your budget estimates. Your campaign plan should list each activity in detail. Estimate costs line by line, from printing for direct mail to office supplies. Most vendors will provide written estimates, and other costs such as postage and advertising rates are either available or easy to calculate.

The overall budget should reflect estimated monthly costs and total costs. Compare your monthly costs and the timing of your campaign activities as outlined in your plan with your fundraising projections. By doing so, you'll be able to determine whether your calendar is in sync with your cash flow.

Here are some budget items to consider:

CAMPAIGN MANAGEMENT
- Manager and media consultant
- Polling
- Legal
- Accounting

HEADQUARTERS
- Rent
- Equipment and supplies
- Insurance
- Utilities
- Phones and fax
- Copiers and computers

GENERAL ADMINISTRATIVE/MEDIA

· Postage
· Stationery and endorsement cards
· Media
· House signs
· Outdoor signs
· Bus stops and billboards
· Neighborhood newspaper ads
· Slate cards
· Photography
· Internet
· Newsletters
· Door hangers
· Walk piece (campaign literature designed to be distributed to voters in-person)
· Direct mail
· Count book and data (breaks down numbers of voters into various geographic and demographic categories)

FIELD

· Field director
· Organizer
· Vote by mail
· Paid phones (phone banks in which calls are made by paid professionals rather than volunteers)
· Get-out-the-vote phones
· Food and supplies
· Database operator

FUNDRAISING

· Fundraising consultant
· Mailing costs
· Event costs

RAISING MONEY

Anyone who has worked for a nonprofit organization or civic cause understands the importance of money in fulfilling a mission. Money is also an important (albeit sometimes unpopular) part of campaigning, allowing you to communicate your message and persuade your swing voters. It may not be everything (a well-worded ballot question, free press, and volunteers can go a long way), but money vastly improves your chances for success at the ballot box.

Estimate what you need to win and determine how to raise the money. As discussed in the budget section, you should have high and low monetary projections that depend on the success of the fundraising program. (Unlike candidate campaigns, there are no contribution or expenditure limits for ballot measure campaigns.) If you can't raise enough to meet your low projections and be competitive, reassess your decision to wage the campaign or propose the measure. It may be better to hold off and take more time to build support and resources.

Before you ask for money, be informed and be prepared. That means understanding the legal issues discussed in detail in the previous section, and it means designing a fundraising plan that outlines the overall strategy and specific techniques for raising the money. An assessment of potential donors is critical; consider any group or individuals who may contribute money to a conservation campaign—the "who" and "how much" of your plan. Several factors will determine success in raising money:

> THE FOCUS OF THE MEASURE. Are you trying to protect farmland, water quality, or urban parks? Different types of measures will attract different types of contributors. Be sure to solicit those groups who may indirectly benefit from the measure as well as those who will directly benefit.

THE LEVEL OF SUPPORT. Do you have the support of a high-level political figure, such as a mayor or a U.S. senator? Do you have the support of a high-profile local leader or celebrity? These individuals can raise the profile of the campaign and raise money from their supporters.

THE FISCAL CONSTRAINTS OF A COMMUNITY. What is the financial picture of a community and how large is its potential pool of contributors? Be realistic about the financial resources available.

OTHER COMPETING MEASURES. Are there other measures on the ballot that may compete for financial resources? Consider the types of contributors these measures may attract.

So who gives to conservation campaigns? Any group or individual who cares about quality of life is a potential donor. A broad pool to consider, no doubt, but it is better to be inclusive from the start and devise your strategy accordingly.

Conservation and environmental groups are an obvious choice; national organizations such as the Trust for Public Land and The Nature Conservancy, the Sierra Club, the Audubon Society, Ducks Unlimited, and the League of Conservation Voters can contribute funds, help raise additional money, and provide strategic fundraising support. Two-thirds of all contributions needed to pass a $125 million park bond in Georgia's DeKalb County in 2001 came from conservation groups such as TPL, The Nature Conservancy, and the Conservation Fund.

Also consider park and recreation associations and other professional organizations. Contributors to a California land and water protection bond (Proposition 40) in 2002 included the California Park and Recreation Society, the Park Rangers Association, and the Parks Hospitality Association, among others.

Local land trusts and community foundations can help. Community foundations can give to ballot measure campaigns and frequently support the early stages of the conservation vision or measure design process by funding research, polls, and other needs.

New parks create new jobs for city workers and other businesses. If your measure is designed to revitalize urban parks and green spaces, add businesses, business groups (such as the chamber of commerce), and municipal unions to your list of potential donors. If your measure creates funding for the purchase of easements on agricultural land, potential donors may include the nonprofit American Farmland Trust, the Farm Bureau, and Cattleman's Association, and for-profit entities such as the wine industry, farmers, and other growers. Many corporations make sizable contributions to support the community. And advertising agencies and law firms can provide pro bono services as well as cash.

Landowners, developers, builders, and Realtor associations can also help. These groups understand that open space is an attractive amenity that preserves quality of life and protects land values. Cape Cod Realtors and conservationists joined forces to help pass a property-tax-funded land bank in 1998. This collaboration was a turning point for the two groups who once fought on either side of a proposed real-estate transfer tax.

Finally, individual supporters can make significant contributions and solicit funds from their friends, colleagues, and other contacts. These "conservation philanthropists" may be business leaders, community leaders, or political leaders with extensive networks who are committed to the conservation cause. They may also be neighborhood activists and residents who are willing to make an investment in their community and their quality of life.

Cast as wide a net as possible: pull contributor lists from past environmental measures, have your finance committee and key supporters compile a list of personal contacts, organize house parties, and ask elected officials to ask their supporters. (Elected officials can also make contributions from their political campaign committees.)

So where can't you get funding? Private foundations, anonymous donors, and government agencies are prohibited from contributing. And remember that contributions to a campaign committee are not tax deductible. This fact must be disclosed in every fundraising solicitation.

THE FINANCE COMMITTEE

No one can raise enough money for a campaign single-handedly. A fundraising coordinator and a finance committee are essential. It is the job of the fundraising coordinator to help develop and execute the fundraising plan and coordinate the activities of the finance committee.

Like the advisory committee, members of the finance committee must be respected in their communities and committed to protecting the land. They should represent the diversity of the jurisdiction. Committee members should be expected to make a monetary contribution to the campaign and to raise money. Members should have ample community experience and professional contacts from which they can solicit donations, and they should be able to enlist the help of others in the fundraising effort. (Finance committee and advisory committee members can overlap. However, try to recruit new people to serve on your finance committee; members of each

CASE STUDY: DEKALB COUNTY CAMPAIGN BEATS THE CLOCK

Campaign leaders in DeKalb County, outside Atlanta, raised $120,000 during a two-month campaign to pass a $125 million green space bond in March 2001. Property taxes were raised to pay for the bond, which would largely fund the purchase of parkland. With lots of momentum but little time, the campaign implemented the following fundraising strategy:

PARTNER WITH NONPROFIT CONSERVATION GROUPS. National and local organizations became partners in the campaign, contributing the majority of funds and advising on campaign strategy.

PUT POPULAR POLITICAL LEADERS FRONT AND CENTER. Newly elected CEO Vernon Jones championed the effort, bringing key supporters and contributors on board and attending fundraising events. An endorsement of the measure from former Lt. Governor Pierre Howard was also helpful in raising money.

ASSEMBLE A FINANCE COMMITTEE. A small but influential finance committee was assembled. Members contributed funds, solicited funds, and asked givers to identify still others. This group was led by a prominent local attorney with connections to the development community, some of whom contributed to the campaign.

Owing to the success of the fundraising effort, the campaign was able to communicate its message with lawn signs, on radio, on cable television, through direct mail, on a web site, and with email. A successful grassroots campaign was also launched.

---

committee will have plenty to do.) Some likely finance committee candidates are as follows: executive director of the local land trust and other environmental organizations, leader of a sports league or recreation association, business leader, local elected official. Keep in mind that the more diverse your members, the broader will be your reach with various parts of the community and constituency groups.

FUNDRAISING TECHNIQUES

With a potential donor list in hand, determine the best approach to raising the money. First, estimate how much each potential donor can give: $50 or less; $50 to $100; $100 to $250; $250 to $500; $500 or more. Those asking for money should have a fundraising packet that contains a fact sheet, brochure, endorsement list, campaign plan overview and fundraising projections, and news clips. Brief fundraisers on the legal issues such as how checks should be written and the need to inform contributors that donations are not tax deductible.

CASE STUDY: CALIFORNIA CONSERVATION MEASURE ATTRACTS WIDESPREAD SUPPORT

Intense development pressures threaten California's last remaining wild landscapes and water resources. To permanently protect its natural resources, California voters have been asked to pass several multibillion-dollar bond measures since 2000, including the $2.6 billion Clean Water, Clean Air, Safe Neighborhood Parks and Coastal Protection Act in March 2002. This measure, called Proposition 40, is helping to fund the acquisition of major properties along the Big Sur coastline, old-growth redwood forests in northern California, watersheds critical to the survival of salmon, the creation of new urban parks and recreational facilities, and the restoration of historical and cultural resources.

The campaign to pass the measure involved a coalition of partners, including state political leaders, nonprofit conservation and environmental organizations, cultural and historical societies, local land trusts, and many others. More than $7 million was raised to send the campaign's message on television and radio, through direct mail, over the web, and with community outreach and direct voter contact.

Several separate committees were formed to support Proposition 40, including the campaign's "Yes on Proposition 40" committee. These entities were established by conservation organizations to help raise campaign contributions (often from their own members) and included The Nature Conservancy Action Fund, TPL's California Conservation Campaign, and the Conservation Action Fund (sponsored by the Planning and Conservation League). The California Conservation Campaign is an offshoot of The Conservation Campaign—TPL's a 501(c)(4) lobbying affiliate that raises money for state and local conservation ballot measures and legislative lobbying programs.

By including a wide array of conservation and related projects, Proposition 40 attracted a diverse group of contributors. Major donors fell into the following groups:

Park and open space protection provides myriad benefits, such as improving the local economy, the environment, public health, and quality of life. Understand the issues that are most important to your audience and tailor your message appropriately. Then determine the best approach to take for each potential donor: personal solicitation, fundraising event, or direct mail.

STATE AND NATIONAL NONPROFIT CONSERVATION ORGANIZATIONS. The Nature Conservancy contributed more than $2.5 million to Proposition 40. Another major donor included TPL's California Conservation Campaign.

ENVIRONMENTAL, PLANNING, AND OTHER CONSERVATION ORGANIZATIONS. Contributors included Ducks Unlimited, the Sierra Club, and the California League of Conservation Voters. The Planning and Conservation League's committee, the Conservation Action Fund, contributed almost $500,000.

LOCAL LAND TRUSTS. The Peninsula Open Space Trust contributed $900,000, making the organization the second-largest Proposition 40 contributor.

PARK AND RECREATION ASSOCIATIONS AND DISTRICTS. Contributors included the California State Parks Foundation, the California Park and Recreation Society, and regional recreation districts, among others.

LANDOWNERS. Landowners who are interested in the protection of land for conservation purposes were major supporters.

MUSEUMS. By including funding for many state museums, Proposition 40 attracted support from museums and historical societies throughout the state.

CORPORATIONS. Contributions from major corporations such as Chevron/Texaco were important to the campaign.

INDIAN TRIBES. The protection of tribal lands drew support from Native American groups.

CAMPAIGN COMMITTEES. Key legislative sponsors of the measure donated funds from their campaign committees. (Although the rules vary from state to state, a candidate's campaign committee can typically donate funds to other campaigns, whereas ballot measure campaigns may spend their money only for their own effort.)

No matter which technique you use to raise the money, always be sure to follow up with a personal and timely thank-you. Make sure donors understand the importance of their contribution—whether it is $5 or $500. And keep in touch with them throughout the campaign, through your fundraising and field programs. Remember, donors are also voters, potential volunteers, and potential future donors.

Personal solicitations. Whether asking for a vote or for a donation, personal contact is effective. The fundraising coordinator, the finance committee, and other key supporters should use this approach whenever possible. For those new to the fundraising process, round up tips for soliciting money, scripts, and role-playing activities to help them.

Personal solicitation can be done by phone, mail, or in person. Some pointers to keep in mind:

· Be honest about the purpose of the call or meeting: to discuss raising money for the conservation measure.

· Explain why the measure is important to the community and might be important to the individual (for example, more parks for children to play in; clean, safe water; or better quality of life, which can mean more tourism and new businesses).

· Provide a verbal outline and written copy of the campaign strategy and fundraising projections.

· Provide a list of supportive individuals and organizations.

· Ask for a specific contribution amount. Or ask donors to underwrite a specific part of the campaign, say, the cost of letterhead or a printer. This type of dedicated gift gives donors an understanding of their investment.

· Ask for names and phone numbers of other people
who might be willing to donate to the campaign. Find
out if your contact would be willing to solicit these
people; if not, ask if you can say you were referred by
your primary contact.

Direct mail. Direct mail fundraising is an expensive, time-
consuming, and involved process. You also need lots of potential
donor lists to make the approach profitable. For these reasons,
direct mail is not typically used for small campaigns. Before
you try to raise money with direct mail, carefully assess your
resources, the costs of mailing, and your time. Costs can include
lists, design and production, and postage.

That said, direct mail can be lucrative for larger campaigns. If
you decide to raise money with direct mail, here are some tips:

· Consider all types of lists. Lists of potential donors, called
"cold" lists, can be purchased from list vendors. They can
consist of past contributors to other conservation causes
or members of "friendly" organizations. Keep in mind the
difference between cold lists and in-house lists. Cold lists
will likely yield significantly fewer responses than an in-
house list of donors who have given in the past. A rate of
return of about 2 percent is typical for cold lists.

· If you're doing a large mailing (500 or more pieces),
consider pretesting your lists. Send out a small percentage
(10 to 20 percent) and wait about three weeks for the
returns. The money you receive will give you an idea of
whether the cost of mailing the rest is worthwhile.

· Tailor your appeal appropriately. The content of the
letter and the name(s) of signer(s) should be appropriate
to the audience.

· Personalized letters are more effective (and more expensive) than "Dear Friend" letters.

· Include a return envelope and consider prepaying the postage if you have the funds.

· Consider making follow-up phone calls if you have the volunteer resources.

For any contribution you receive, be sure to send a prompt thank-you letter. Also be sure to keep contributors' names for future solicitations and get-out-the-vote.

Fundraising events. Fundraising events can help energize donors and keep them informed about the campaign. The events themselves can be big-ticket ($100 plus per person), small-ticket ($25 or less per person), or somewhere in between. Determine your prices according to the type of invitee. You can also solicit different levels of donations from different guests; big givers can be listed as patrons or friends. The type of event—an outdoor barbeque, a wine and cheese reception—should also be reflective of the ticket prices. The key to fundraising events is to keep your costs down. Try to get donations for food, entertainment, and venue. You may want to ask supporters and advisory committee members to purchase a minimum number of tickets. They can then resell them or incur the cost.

House parties are another kind of fundraising event, one that combines raising money with grassroots organizing. In these parties, neighbors invite neighbors from all corners of the community. The parties are small-ticket events and serve to inform people about the campaign, identify supporters, and enlist future volunteers.

CASE STUDY: SMALL CHECKS ADD UP TO BIG SUPPORT IN BOISE

Many campaigns only claim to be grassroots, but in Boise, Idaho, that description fits. To protect the Boise Foothills, hundreds of volunteers supported the one paid staffer—the campaign manager—by coordinating events, the field program, media, and fundraising activities. Of the 1,000 campaign contributions, only two were from outside Boise.

Although there was some business support, most of the money came from individuals. And many of these were small checks: the campaign held 20 house parties in two months, raising $20,000 from checks of $25 or less. Overall, the campaign raised twice as much as expected, allowing it to respond to attacks by opponents with messages on radio, with prerecorded phone calls, and in direct mail. The $10 million open space protection program was approved with 60 percent of the vote in May 2001.

PHOTO BY FRANK L. BALTHIS

VOTER SUPPORT FOR SEVERAL MULTIBILLION-DOLLAR BOND MEASURES HAS HELPED PROTECT THE CALIFORNIA COASTLINE.

Consider including house parties as part of your field and fundraising plans. Supporters who host house parties should be given plenty of information about the campaign to distribute. A campaign representative should be there to address the group, answer questions, and sign up volunteers.

SECURING ENDORSEMENTS

St. Louis's Proposition C campaign for Clean Water, Safe Parks and Community Trails enjoyed the support of political leaders like former U.S. Senator John C. Danforth and national celebrities (and area residents) like Bob Costas and Jackie Joyner-Kersee. Their endorsements on direct mail pieces increased the measure's profile and appeal. While you may not have such big-name celebrities on hand, you can turn to trusted influential community leaders and respected organizations with good name recognition.

You may have tested the public's trust in some organizations and individuals in your poll. These results will tell you which of these high-level people—such as mayor, supervisor, local land trust—can move swing voters. If you haven't polled or can't test every potential endorsement in your poll, brainstorm with your advisory committee and campaign staff about what other endorsements could help your measure.

Try to line up key endorsements early—during the measure development phase if possible. Include top-level public officials and community leaders in the campaign process. Just as you organized your finance committee, have your advisory committee members reach out to the people they know. These members and the campaign manager can set up meetings with potential endorsers, provide them with a packet of information (fact sheet, news clips, campaign plan), and brief them on the measure. Ask for endorsements directly and make sure to get it in writing; endorsers should sign a card stating their support and giving their permission to use their name in campaign materials.

Organizers for a measure to expand the Open Space and Farmland Preservation Trust Fund in Morris County, New Jersey, lined up endorsements from nearly all of the state and county political leaders representing their community. Included were all seven of the county's freeholders as well as a majority of the county's representatives in the state senate and assembly. Nearly 30 organizations also backed the measure, including national, state, and local conservation organizations and a state tax watchdog group. The campaign committee included prominent leaders in business, conservation, and government, including former Governor Thomas Kean. Their early support helped jump-start other campaign activities, including endorsements and fundraising.

Finally, you may want to secure endorsements from as many voters as possible. A list of several hundred supporters speaks volumes about the depth of your grassroots campaign. Volunteers can gather names of supporters as part of your field organization. Simply instruct phoners and walkers to ask identified supporters if they are willing to be listed as an endorser in printed materials. Those who agree should sign an endorsement card.

> # YES! I support Prop A for
> # clean water & open space!
> ❑ You may use my name publicly as an endorser
> ❑ I want to volunteer on the campaign by:
>   ❑ Putting up a house sign   ❑ Telephoning voters   ❑ Fundraising
>   ❑ Walking my precinct   ❑ Hosting a house party   ❑ Other, please call
> Name _____
> Home Address_____
> Occupation_____
> Phone (evening)_____ (day)_____
> email_____ For more information call 999-9999
>   or visit www.cleanwater.com

AN ENDORSEMENT CARD CAN GATHER INFORMATION ABOUT HOW A SUPPORTER WANTS TO HELP THE CAMPAIGN.

It may be important to demonstrate the breadth of your support in printed materials or through the free or paid media. For instance, you may want to distribute neighborhood-specific fact sheets that list area supporters. Or you may want to print a hundred names on the back of one of your direct mail pieces.

DEVELOPING A PAID MEDIA PLAN

Paid media advertising allows you to clearly communicate and control your message. The content, timing, and placement of these ads can be targeted to reach your swing voters, making them an invaluable part of any campaign. On the downside, paid media is expensive and is considered less credible than communication through the free media or volunteer outreach.

Frequent voters living in the St. Louis metro region heard about Proposition C several times in the fall of 2000. First, they received information in the mail: the campaign distributed several different direct mail pieces highlighting the measure's park safety and recreation benefits. While the campaign spanned six counties in Missouri and Illinois, plus the city of St. Louis, these pieces were tailored to provide residents of each jurisdiction with information about improvements to their local parks. Voters heard about clean, safe parks on their car radios: Prop C radio ads were placed on targeted stations, those with predominantly African-American listeners. And voters tuned into Prop C on their televisions, seeing ads that highlighted land protection benefits repeatedly in the final weeks of the campaign.

Campaign advisors in St. Louis understood the impact of paid media and how to target their messages and resources effectively. While you may not have the resources to do television, radio, and direct mail, carefully consider the various types of paid media and incorporate what you can into your campaign. Advertising for land conservation can be particularly powerful; people have strong, emotional attachments to the land that can be communicated in print or broadcast media. Use these to tell your story, convey the facts, and persuade voters of the merits of your measure.

Paid media advertising includes direct mail, newspaper, television, radio, signs, and billboards. Just which of these (or which combination) to use depends on a variety of factors, including campaign strategy, budget, advertising costs, size and composition of the jurisdiction, types of media available, and the swing voter audience. For example, to attract the attention of elected leaders and potential donors early on in the campaign, a full-page newspaper ad might be the best method. If you have limited cash and limited time, you might decide to do two direct mail pieces to a narrowly targeted group of voters in the week before election day.

To use paid media to the best advantage, consider these questions:

· What types of paid media make sense? If your jurisdiction is a small part of a large television media market, for instance, it probably doesn't make sense to advertise on television.

· Which messages need to reach which voters? You may decide to reach a broad audience through high-impact, emotional messages on television or radio. Alternatively, you can send more specific messages to more defined groups of voters through the mail.

· Should you run a high- or low-profile campaign? You may
need to attract attention early to generate endorsements
or raise money; paid media can help. On the other hand,
you may want to avoid generating debate or opposition by
using communications that garner less public attention,
such as direct mail.

· How much money will you have? Budget for repetition
and impact. For example, three direct mail pieces to a
targeted group of swing voters are usually better than
one piece to all likely voters.

Weigh all of these factors and then design a strategy that gives
you the best value for the highest impact with your targeted voters.
Design ads that compel voters to support your measure. And
carefully coordinate your paid media to complement the other
components of the campaign (you'll likely want to save most of
your paid media until the end of the campaign when voters are
paying the most attention). The review of each type of paid media
in the following pages will help you understand the strength of
each approach and the process by which it is implemented.

DESIGNING DIRECT MAIL

To political consultants, direct mail is one of the most cost-effective ways to communicate targeted messages to swing voters. Imagine the possibilities:

· A letter from a senior group assuring likely voters over age 60 that the measure is well designed and cost effective

· A brochure about youth recreational opportunities to two-parent households

· An endorsement card from a popular Democratic official to likely Democratic voters urging them to vote for your measure on election day

Whatever the strategy, use direct mail to send powerful, targeted messages to key voting groups.

If you're a regular voter, your mailbox is probably filled with political direct mail at election time. How much time do you spend on each piece—a couple of minutes, a couple of seconds? Be sure to design pieces that grab the reader's attention and communicate your message succinctly and persuasively.

Fortunately, land conservation is an issue that can attract attention; images of treasured lands or sprawl and degradation can be powerful in direct mail, newspaper, or television advertising. If a particular piece of land, animal, forest, lake, or river evokes strong emotions in your community, use its image throughout your mail.

TYPES OF DIRECT MAIL

There are several different types of direct mail to consider. Persuasion mail does just that—persuades targeted voters, through words and images, to support your measure. A letter from an elected official, a postcard highlighting endorsements, a full-color brochure filled with photos of threatened lands—all of this is persuasion mail.

Persuasion mail is also used to increase absentee ballot voting among targeted groups. Absentee ballots are a good way to lock in votes among likely supporting groups early. If the rules in your state allow you to send applications for absentee ballots in the mail, include messages on the application form and send them to identified or likely supporters. These messages should reinforce the need to support your measure and vote by mail. Then, time your other direct mail pieces so that absentee ballot voters receive your persuasion mail before they vote. Be sure to determine the percentage of the electorate that typically votes absentee and allocate your direct mail resources to reflect that number. (See page 177 for information about absentee ballot programs.)

Educational mail, as opposed to persuasion mail, informs voters about a measure without asking them to vote yes. Most public agencies and foundations are prevented from using their funds for campaign purposes. However, an agency may be able to educate the public about a measure without advocating for it. (In some cases state law may prohibit its governments from any sort of communication regarding a ballot question.) The McHenry County Conservation Foundation in McHenry County, Illinois, produced an effective educational piece about the open space general obligation bond measure on the November 2000 ballot. The four-color piece included photos of the recreational opportunities in the district, ballot measure wording, and basic facts about the measure. While it didn't ask voters to support the measure, it did ask them to "take a close look at the referendum and give it your best consideration."

SOURCE: THE STRATEGY GROUP

AN IMPORTANT CAMPAIGN MESSAGE IN SANTA FE: PROTECTING OUR RIVERS, STREAMS, AND AQUIFERS ENSURES OUR CHILDREN HAVE SAFE AND CLEAN DRINKING WATER.

SOURCE: BATES NIEMAND

THE PROTECTION OF A COMMUNITY'S FARMING AND RANCHING HERITAGE CAN BE COMPELLING TO VOTERS IN RURAL AREAS.

SOURCE: THE STRATEGY GROUP
PROTECTING QUALITY OF LIFE BY
PRESERVING NATURAL AREAS AND
FARMLAND WAS AN IMPORTANT ISSUE
FOR RESIDENTS OF THIS FAST-GROWING
MINNESOTA COUNTY.

Other printed materials to consider are campaign letter-head, door hangers, and lawn/house signs. Supporters and volunteers typically love campaign paraphernalia like buttons, bumper stickers, and pens. These do little to help communicate your message to targeted voters, however, and will use up limited funds.

DIRECT MAIL PRODUCTION

Here are some things to consider when designing and implementing your direct mail program:

PLAN AHEAD. Map out your pieces—format and content, targeted universe, and production timing—in a direct mail plan early in your campaign. Almost invariably there will be a holdup somewhere along the line: a lengthy approval process, pieces that are slow to print, a direct mail company that is behind schedule, or a post office that sits on your mail. Build in several extra days to account for the unknown.

GET AN ACCURATE LIST OF VOTERS. Lists of "voter counts" can be obtained from a list vendor—a private, for-profit company that maintains voter files. Voter counts provide voter turnout figures and the number of voters in various categories (seniors, Republicans, women, and so on). Voter count sheets are typically provided free of charge with the expectation that voter lists—the actual names, addresses, or phone numbers of voters (for paid media and field campaigning)—will be purchased once strategic campaign decisions are made. Voter counts will tell you how many voters are in each subset, allowing you to target and budget your direct mail accordingly. When you're ordering mailing labels, make sure to "household" them—that is, group your voters by household rather than by individual. This will save you the added cost of sending two or more mail pieces to one home.

CONCEPT, COPY, AND PHOTOS SHOULD BE COMPELLING. Use photos and language that convey the importance of protecting land, providing recreational opportunities, or limiting sprawl, depending on your campaign message. Don't say too much: communicate important factual information without overloading the voter. Work with a professional graphic designer to create your pieces, but before you produce them, make sure the post office will mail the format you select and determine the postage costs. Standard formats, with various folds, are 8 ½ x 11 (one-fold or postcard); 11 x 17; 11 x 22; and 5 ½ x 8 ½ postcard. Check out the U.S. Postal Service web site (www.usps.gov) for a complete rundown on mailing sizes and weights.

LINE UP YOUR VENDORS. Find reputable printers (local trade associations can be helpful) and direct mail firms. Consider the value of using union printers and printing the pieces on recycled paper with soy ink. Outline the scope of the print job: piece specifications, quantity, paper stock, number of colors, turnaround time. Outline the scope of the direct mail job: piece specifications, quantity, drop-date. Request written price quotes.

TIME YOUR PIECES CAREFULLY. When to drop your mail depends on your campaign strategy and mail budget. If you're mailing only a piece or two, drop as close to election day as possible (but not too close to risk missing election day altogether). If your direct mail plan includes numerous pieces to different target groups, spread these out over the course of weeks, or even months. Time these pieces to reflect current events whenever possible.

THE MECHANICS OF BULK MAILING

Except for the occasional first-class letter, your pieces will probably all be classified as bulk mail. Sending mail in bulk, rather than first class, saves about 30 percent on postage, and that savings increases the bigger the quantity of the mailing. You may decide to print a "walk piece," which will be distributed door to door only. But to be safe, print your bulk mail permit on the walk pieces. If you have extra cash, you may decide to mail some as well.

In order to plan accordingly, it is important to understand how political bulk mail works and to know postal rules and regulations. Your direct mail firm will deliver or "drop" your mail at the appropriate bulk mail facility, which will then "red-tag" the mail bags, indicating political direct mail. Legally, the post office is required to treat political direct mail as first class, making it a priority over other direct mail. From there it is sorted and delivered to the appropriate post offices and on to voters' homes.

The length of the process will vary. Some mail will move through the bulk mail facility and the post offices in one day; most mail will arrive at voters' homes within two to three days. Some post offices, however, move more slowly than others. And some post offices and bulk mail facilities get jammed with political mail during the days just before an election. Try to find out about the efficiency of the bulk mail facility and post offices in your community. A good source of information is your direct mail firm, whose job it is to work with the post offices. Be prepared to track your mail. That means establishing a relationship with a supervisor in the bulk mail facility and pushing to get the mail out in a timely manner. If your schedule is tight, it is helpful to visit the facility in person when the mail arrives. Follow through to make sure it is processed and distributed as quickly as possible. From there you may need to contact each post office.

There are two ways to obtain a bulk mail permit. First, you can apply at the post office. The post office will give you your permit number; be sure to find out the exact wording and size for the bulk mail indicia that must be printed on each piece so that you can instruct your designer. You must also fill out a form for the post office for each mailing and write a check to cover the postage amount.

The other alternative is to use your direct mail firm's bulk mail indicia. This will save you the cost and hassle of getting your own permit, but one possible disadvantage is the address. The indicia typically reads "US Postage Paid, City Name, State, Permit #." If your direct mail firm is located outside the community you're campaigning in, you may want to obtain your own mailing permit with an address within the jurisdiction.

The post office discounts bulk mailings because you (or your direct mail firm) do some of the work for them, such as sorting

SOURCE: THE TRUST FOR PUBLIC LAND

THIS MAIL PIECE COMMUNICATED TO VOTERS THE IMPORTANCE OF PROTECTING "THE RIVERS" IN ORMOND BEACH, FLORIDA.

or delivering to a bulk mail facility. Postage costs will depend on the format of the piece and the quantity of the mailing. Call your nearest bulk mail facility to obtain an up-to-date rate sheet. With this information you can estimate postage costs for your direct mail budget.

Nonprofit postal rates are even further discounted. TPL and TCC may send only their own mail at the special nonprofit bulk rates, meaning they must devise, design, and pay for the pieces. All mailings must identify the sponsoring organization with its address.

ADVERTISING IN THE NEWSPAPER

Newspaper ads can be used to persuade readers, communicate endorsements, and/or get-out-the-vote. Determine your objectives for advertising in the newspaper: Is it important to reach community leaders with your message or generate a buzz about your campaign? Would a newspaper ad complement articles or editorials that you anticipate? Are there weeklies or ethnic papers that can reach a targeted audience?

Many major cities now have only one major newspaper, often with circulations in excess of 100,000. In these cases, advertising can be expensive and targeting is difficult.[31] These newspapers can, however, reach a broad audience (including a community's decision-makers) with high-impact, persuasive messages and images. Figure out the audiences and circulations for all area newspapers, daily and weekly. Try to assess the significance of a newspaper within a community and the political persuasion of its editorial board. Don't forget to consider the smaller, suburban dailies, which often place more emphasis on local issues and attract the readers you need to reach.

Advertising in weeklies and ethnic newspapers (which are typically weekly) can also be a cost-effective way to reach targeted voter groups.

Your paid media strategy should outline the purpose of newspaper advertising, best timing and content of ads, and costs. On the production side, you must determine each newspaper's formats, ad rates, deadlines, and run dates. Here are some things to consider:

> FORMAT. Look at the ads and note which size you think you'll need to effectively communicate your message within your budget: full-page, half-page, quarter-page. Standard format is by column inches per page, so a one-inch ad across one column is a column inch. A full-page ad would be six columns, each about 21 inches long, or 126 column inches. Find out all the details of the ad format: In which software program should the ad be designed? Do they accept only camera-ready art? How should the ad be sent (electronically or in the mail)? The newspaper advertising department can provide you with production guidelines that outline the format. Newspaper advertising departments often provide design services for free. If you can't afford a graphic designer, consider this approach.

> RATES. Most newspapers have a standard rate per column inch, but some will offer discounts for larger purchases. Political ad rates are typically lower than commercial rates, so be sure to have an ad rep send you a rate sheet for political ads.

> DEADLINES. Newspapers have strict deadlines. Determine early when the ad needs to reach the newspaper and to whom it needs to go. Typically, a newspaper requires that the ad be ready a couple of days before publication.

SOURCE: THE TRUST FOR PUBLIC LAND

THESE NEWSPAPER ADS COMMUNICATED KEY CAMPAIGN MESSAGES IN PITKIN
COUNTY, COLORADO, AND MECKLENBURG COUNTY, NORTH CAROLINA. BOTH
MEASURES WERE SUCCESSFUL

RUN DATES. Keep in mind that Sunday circulations are generally the largest (and most expensive). Saturday and Monday papers are often less well read. Make sure each newspaper sends you copies of the ad once it has appeared.

PRODUCING BROADCAST MEDIA

ADVERTISING ON TELEVISION

Television is a powerful medium, and land conservation proponents can use it effectively to convey the importance of protecting open space, keeping water clean, or preventing sprawl. Television is also expensive and difficult to target. (Cable television is an alternative that can help with both issues, but its reach is also limited.) And television is memorable and high profile, attracting attention for your measure in a way that direct mail does not.

If you have the budget for television, you probably have the budget to hire a professional to produce the spots and buy your airtime. If you can't afford one, your local cable company may be able to provide production services.

Spots are generally 30 seconds in length. With limited time it is essential to communicate your message clearly and creatively in a way that will move swing voters. Be sure to include your required legal disclaimer at the end of the spot. Disclaimer requirements vary by state but typically require the words "paid for by the [committee name]" across the screen.

Repetition is the key to effective electronic media, just as it is with direct mail. Budget your resources to buy a sufficient number of gross rating points. These points are a measure of a program's viewership—the higher the rating, the more people

TELEVISION SCRIPTS
PROPOSITION C, ST. LOUIS, NOVEMBER 2000
(30 SECONDS)

SPOT #1

Safe water, clean parks, nature.

Things we enjoy with our children every day.

We can protect and preserve these precious resources with Proposition C.

Prop C will protect and improve water quality, clean up our parks, preserve natural lands for wildlife, and conserve our open spaces.

And Prop C will have annual independent audits to make sure the money is spent properly.

Prop C. You'll see the difference.

SPOT #2

Water.

From the majestic Mississippi, to Lake St. Louis, to the simple faucet in our kitchen, water is an essential part of our daily lives.

To safeguard our water and the people who use it, Proposition C will protect parks and land around our waterways to improve water quality.

But that's not all. Prop C will have annual independent audits to make sure the money is spent properly.

Proposition C. You'll see the difference.

Paid for by the TPL Land Action Fund; Ernest Cook, president.

SOURCE: DOAK, CARRIER, AND O'DONNELL

are watching the program and your spot. For instance, if a program has a rating of 20, an estimated 20 percent of the viewing audience is watching. One ad during the program brings in 20 points. As a general guideline, you should budget a minimum of 500 to 1,000 points. If you are buying less than 1,000 points, do not air more than one spot.

You can get rates and demographic data from each broadcast station and your local cable stations. Carefully consider the most efficient way to reach swing voters. For instance, buying news prime time will cost more than daytime because the ad reaches more people. Yet prime time also attracts nonvoters (under 18 years old) and may be less effective than morning, daytime, or news times.

ADVERTISING ON RADIO

Radio allows you to convey emotion and tell a story. You won't be able to target your audience as effectively as with direct mail, but you can target it more accurately than with television at a reduced cost. As with other mediums, go for repetition: by some estimates, a person must hear a radio spot 25 times before the message sinks in.[32]

If you're considering a radio buy, first get a listing of radio stations in your media market. Request a rate card for each station (make sure you ask for political rates, which are generally the lowest rates in any time slot) along with listener demographic data. Find the stations with the demographics that most closely reflect your targeted voter categories—older voters, African-American voters, Spanish-speaking voters, and so on. Try to buy spots early; popular drive-time news adjacency spots go quickly, particularly during campaign season.

Ads are typically 30 or 60 seconds in length. Your ad can be produced at the station (for a cost and using the station's talent) or in a studio of your choice. You'll probably want to hire a professional "voice." Local talent agents can provide you with demo tapes. You may also want to consider using a personality from a local radio station.

RADIO SCRIPT
SANTA FE COUNTY, NOVEMBER 2000
(60 SECONDS)

Sound effects: We hear the sounds of a babbling brook fade under a music bed.

Female voice: The hot, dry summer we just experienced was a wake-up call reminding us how precious water is in Santa Fe County. As communities grow, it is critically important to protect our watersheds from development to ensure a steady source of clean water.

In 1998, Santa Fe County voters passed the first Wildlife, Mountain Trails, and Historic Places bond. That money, now nearly spent, allowed us to purchase and protect watersheds and thousands of acres of mountains and foothills rich in sacred petroglyphs and wildlife.

But much of our watershed is still in danger of being lost to development forever. That's why we need your vote November 7th for a new bond—Santa Fe County Bond C—so we can finish the job we started.

To guarantee a legacy of stunning landscapes and historic treasures for our children and grandchildren and protect the watersheds that provide clean water, please vote "YES" on Santa Fe County Bond C.

Paid for by New Mexicans to Protect Our Watersheds, a project of the TPL Land Action Fund, Ted Harrison, chair.

SOURCE: NEW WEST POLICY GROUP

POSTING HOUSE SIGNS
AND BILLBOARDS

House signs can give your measure visibility, improve name recognition, and signal to the public and the press that your campaign is gaining strength, neighborhood by neighborhood. House signs can also help generate awareness and enthusiasm in key precincts.

Before you print and post any political signs, make sure you understand the local laws and regulations governing them:

· What are the size limitations?

· Where can signs be posted?

· When can signs be posted?

· When must they be removed?

· What disclaimer is required?

SOURCE: THE TRUST FOR PUBLIC LAND

A SALES-TAX EXTENSION APPROVED BY VOTERS IN ATHENS-CLARKE COUNTY, GEORGIA, HELPED FUND LAND PRESERVATION ALONG THE OCONEE RIVER.

Carefully evaluate your volunteer resources before launching a sign program. Volunteer precinct captains or walkers can distribute your signs to willing supporters throughout your community. When supporters are identified through the phone or walk program, ask them if they are willing to post a sign. The volunteer who identifies the supporter must make sure the sign is distributed in a timely manner.

In addition, a sign company can post in public spaces for a fee. Make sure the sign company understands the local signage rules, such as when and where political signs can be posted, and be sure that the company is responsible for removing the signs once the election is over.

Make sure your signs are easy to read by the driver of a passing car, are simple but eye-catching, and send one clear message (for example, "Protect Our Land & Water: Vote YES on Prop A").

Billboards are also a useful, albeit pricey way to increase name identification. Make sure to check into availability early. Be aware that rules and regulations vary and that in some communities billboards are not allowed.

WORKING WITH CAMPAIGN CONSULTANTS

Consultants come in all shapes and sizes. Pollsters guide the design and interpret the results of a public opinion poll. Media consultants help design and implement a campaign's paid media plan. Some media consultants specialize in direct mail, while others may offer electronic media expertise. General consultants provide strategic advice and guide the entire operation, from grassroots organizing to free and paid media. Fundraising consultants specialize in raising money for the campaign.

Before hiring a consultant, take a look at your bank account. Consultants may simply be out of reach for many small campaigns—leaving you with effective messages and strategies but no money for implementation. If you have the resources, hire a consultant. But first consider these issues:

ASSESS YOUR NEEDS. You can hire a general consultant to help design your campaign strategy and build your operations. This person is most useful in larger, more expensive races to head a team of professionals and oversee the entire campaign. A media consultant can be critical for all but the smallest campaigns. This professional can help design and implement a paid media strategy—the content, cost, level, and timing of the advertising in the campaign. If your budget is limited, you can also hire professionals to handle various parts of the media process. Typically, these include creative (designing and writing a piece/spot), production, and media buying.

CHECK YOUR BANK ACCOUNT. Consultants can be pricey. Make sure you weigh the costs of a consultant against your estimated budget. Be aware that consultants have a variety of pricing structures: hourly fees, set consulting/creative fees, commissions on advertising, or some combination of these. Consultants generally charge a 15 percent commission on print, television, and radio advertising, although larger campaigns may be able to negotiate lower rates.

LOOK FOR EXPERIENCE. It is helpful, but not mandatory, for a consultant to have worked on land conservation ballot measures before. Look for someone with experience winning races and designing effective media, and find out what experience the consultant has with low-budget campaigns. Check references and review as many media samples from similar campaigns as possible, being sure to assess the strategy in which the media was prepared.

UNDERSTAND THE SCOPE OF RESPONSIBILITIES. Be clear about your expectations and make sure the consultant is prepared to meet them. Depending on the circumstances, your consultant may be needed to review the research and poll, meet with key campaign staff, and/or design a communications strategy.

Work closely with any consultant you hire. It is up to you to keep them on track and up-to-date. Here are some tips for working with the media consultant you've hired:

- Insist on a signed contract. The contract should outline responsibilities and fees.

- Make sure the researcher, pollster, campaign manager, and consultant meet to discuss the overall campaign and paid media strategies. Ideally, a media consultant will be around early enough to participate in the planning process.

- Make sure the consultant's paid media plan complements the rest of the campaign. For instance, paid and free media and field messages need to be coordinated.

- Make sure the consultant has provided details of the types of paid media to be used, the messages and target audiences, the costs, and the timing. Do these work within your budget?

· Understand your responsibilities and the responsibilities of those within the campaign. For instance, the media consultant may provide you with the concept and copy for a direct mail piece. It is up to you (and/or other key campaign advisors or staff) to approve the idea or make changes in a timely manner. If you don't stick to the deadlines, your media will likely be delayed.

· Make sure your consultant is aware of any strategic changes, attacks by the opposition, press coverage, or feedback from the field program. Regular meetings or conference calls are recommended.

MEDIA CONSULTANTS SELL LOTS OF SKILLS: EXPERIENCE, PRODUCTION VALUES, CREATIVITY, STRATEGIC ABILITY, MEDIA-BUYING EXPERTISE AND MORE. ALL ARE IMPORTANT. BUT IN OUR VIEW, THE MOST IMPORTANT QUESTION A [CAMPAIGN] SHOULD ASK OF A MEDIA CONSULTANT IS, DO I TRUST THEM TO TELL MY STORY?

MARK MELLMAN AND MICHAEL BLOOMFIELD
CAMPAIGNS & ELECTIONS MAGAZINE

PLANNING FOR FREE MEDIA

You'll pay a bundle to advertise your message on television, radio, and in the newspaper. Favorable press coverage sends your message for free through an independent, persuasive source— although opposition arguments will likely be included.

Just as for paid media, you should carefully design a free media (sometimes referred to as earned media) strategy and plan. That means determining not only the messages to highlight to the press but also the type and amount of free media you want. Although it may seem like common sense (particularly to enthusiastic supporters) that the more free press coverage the better, this is not always the case with local land conservation campaigns. By resisting the urge to generate early and frequent press coverage, you may also avoid energizing antitax opponents. So carefully assess your opposition and consider delaying your press conferences, op-eds, and letters to the editor until election day nears.

In the case of smaller, lower-profile measures that will not generate much free press attention, your outreach should complement planned coverage by the press. For instance, a local newspaper may not cover much about your race in the weeks preceding the election, but it will probably editorialize about the measure and run a story or two about the campaign in the days just before the election. Make sure you know what is being planned and be prepared to respond accordingly: line up your spokesperson, assemble your press packet, organize your press conference, and prepare for your editorial board meeting. For larger and/or more controversial measures, stories will be written early and often and you must be prepared.

Once a strategy is in place, the press secretary should map out specifics in a free press plan. This plan should outline how and when the campaign's message will be communicated through print and broadcast media—stories, profiles, op-eds, letters to the editor. Here are some pointers:

UNDERSTAND THE BASIC TOOLS. A variety of tools can be used to tell your story through the free media. Press releases can be used to inform the media about an issue, event, endorsement, or other newsworthy subject. Press conferences can tell a story (providing important visual images), highlight key supporters, and share important, breaking news. Op-eds can provide background on an issue and persuade readers about a measure. Letters to the editor and call-in radio forums can demonstrate public support and public perspectives about a measure.

UNDERSTAND THE MEDIA MARKET. Before you can implement any press plan, you must figure out who might cover the measure. Assemble a complete list of television, print, and radio reporters and their phone, fax, email, and mailing information. Include anyone who might talk about your campaign along the way—television news anchors, radio talk show hosts, newspaper columnists. Be sure to include ethnic and weekly newspapers, wire services, and local magazines. Next, assess the most effective free press ways in which to reach your targeted voters. Which radio talk show reaches your demographic audience? Is there a must-read columnist at the daily newspaper? Are there smaller radio stations that will accept radio actualities, which are taped news releases? Understand your audience, prioritize your time, and maximize your most important press opportunities.

INTRODUCE YOURSELF. Get to know the reporters who are covering your campaign, tell them about the measure, and let them know you're available to help them with their stories.

INFORM REPORTERS. Press packets inform reporters about all aspects of the campaign and the measure, including key campaign staff and contact information; a fact sheet about the benefits of the measure to the community; and information on the benefits of land conservation, including the economic impact, positive media coverage to date, and a photo(s) of the land at issue. For larger campaigns, consider mailing or posting on your web site campaign updates that include a recap of weekly developments, positive press coverage, or new information. Increasingly, campaigns are using technology to get their message out. Assess the value of a web site for your campaign. This tool can be an effective way to communicate with reporters, as well as a way to reach voters, supporters, volunteers, and contributors. (See page 166 for more information about Internet campaign strategies.)

LINE UP YOUR SPOKESPEOPLE. The press secretary may serve as spokesperson and/or may coordinate others to speak for the campaign. Potential spokespeople could include elected officials, community leaders, or environmentalists. Assess the strengths of each spokesperson and the types of stories or medium for which they are best suited. These spokespeople should always be well briefed on the reporter and story angle, with talking points in hand. You can also rely on volunteers and supporters to write letters to the editor and op-eds. Make sure these people understand the specific messages that you're trying to convey: provide sample letters, opinions, or talking points to the most credible person on a particular issue—as well as the contact information and deadline for the newspaper.

PLAN YOUR STORIES. If your campaign calls for it, be proactive. Brainstorm as many ways as possible to effectively tell your story. Have members of the local historical society give a tour of a site and talk about its significance to the community. Find parents who can talk about how after-school recreational programs in parks have made a difference in their children's lives. Have supporters in the chamber of commerce talk about the benefits of land conservation to the local economy.

Your press events or press releases can take several different forms: organizational, endorsement, or issue oriented. An "organizational" communication with the press may feature a campaign kickoff rally, highlight fundraising success, or announce key campaign personnel. An endorsement press conference is a place to showcase a broad base of community and political support. Issue-oriented events highlight the benefits of the measure. Consider rolling out different stories, week by week, that complement paid media messages. For instance, hold separate press events that highlight each of the measure's benefits. Back up these events with op-eds and letters to the editor.

RESPOND QUICKLY AND APPROPRIATELY. If a reporter is on the wrong track and opponents attack the measure, set the record straight. Evaluate the most appropriate way to respond to inaccurate coverage (sometimes it is better to let a story die) and utilize the most effective tools (press release, press conference, interview with a spokesperson, and so on).

MONITOR YOUR COVERAGE. Track stories in the press and media. Evaluate their accuracy. Follow up with reporters who have left out critical information or misunderstood the issue. Share positive stories with supporters, potential contributors, other reporters, or with voters through mailings.

TEN TIPS FOR TALKING
WITH A REPORTER

---

1. **BE PREPARED.** Ask the reporter questions. What's your deadline? What kind of story is it? What's your angle? Who else has been or will be interviewed? Learn about the reporter's style and media outlet.

2. **KNOW YOUR STORY.** An interview is an opportunity to tell your story. Select your three key messages. Include facts, figures, and anecdotes to make your story compelling for the audience.

3. **REMEMBER YOUR AUDIENCE.** A news interview is your chance to reach the public or a key audience. Look beyond a reporter's interview techniques and tailor your remarks and demeanor to your audience.

4. **BE ASSERTIVE.** Don't just answer questions; seize every opportunity to drive your messages. Reporters grab their audiences' attention by leading off with the most important, newsworthy information. Do the same thing with each of your answers.

5. **USE FLAGS AND BRIDGES.** Signal that a key point is coming up by flagging it with such phrases as "the key point is" and "what makes this important is." Link each answer to a positive message by using "bridging" phrases such as "but let me put this in perspective" and "but the real problem is."

6. **TURN NEGATIVES TO POSITIVE.** Don't be provoked. Anticipate tough questions and develop responsive answers that are not defensive. Use each question to bridge to one of your key messages.

7. **WHEN YOU DON'T KNOW, SAY SO.** You are an expert, but you don't have all the answers. Say, "I'll get back to you," or "I can put you in touch with someone who has that expertise."

8. **AVOID PROFESSIONAL BUZZWORDS.** The public doesn't know your industry jargon, so don't use it even when the reporter does. Explain abbreviations and technical terms.

9. **FOCUS ON YOUR OBJECTIVE.** Don't get mired in statistics or lengthy explanations. If you want to be quoted, speak briefly and to the point. Correct misstatements and misperceptions.

10. **BEWARE OF INTERVIEWING TRAPS.** Use your own words. Don't repeat negative language or allow the reporter to put words in your mouth. Never lose your cool. Most of all, remember that there is no such thing as off the record.

SOURCE: KETCHUM PUBLIC RELATIONS; COMMUNICATIONS TRAINING CENTER.

DESIGNING AN INTERNET
CAMPAIGN STRATEGY

For large campaigns, the Internet can play an important role facilitating fundraising, communicating with the press, and increasing voter awareness. For smaller campaigns, a web site is probably not cost effective unless it is free. If you can get the costs of the site donated, first make sure you have the volunteer manpower to maintain it.

Advocates for open space protection in Boise, Idaho, launched a web site to promote their measure. The campaign had originally hoped to use the site to solicit volunteer and campaign contributions, but even though the design was donated, they lacked funds to access the necessary technology. Instead they used the site to provide information about the measure, such as costs to taxpayers, open space protection benefits, and voting. In addition, a list of more than 500 email addresses was gathered from the web site and events. Regular messages were distributed to this list to reinforce support, provide campaign updates, remind people to vote, and so on.

PHOTO BY ALYX KELLINGTON

The campaign to pass a $125 million conservation bond in DeKalb County, Georgia, also sent regular email messages to people who visited its web site. Designed and maintained pro bono, the site was used to provide information and solicit contributors and volunteers.

Here are some advantages and disadvantages of a campaign web site:

· A web site can help you communicate information about your campaign with the public, the press, and supporters. Detailed information can be posted quickly, giving the campaign an ability to react to new developments and giving supporters the tools to spread the message. "Grass roots isn't just about door-to-door; it's about friend-to-friend," notes political Internet strategist Becky Donatelli.[33] "The Internet has the potential to arm voters with the information they need to talk to their friends and promote substantive discussion of the issues." The Internet does not, however, replace direct voter contact. Web sites are excellent vehicles to share information, but traditional tools such as direct mail or grassroots voter contact give assurance that persuasion messages are reaching your targeted voters.

· A web site allows for two-way communication with voters. Opinions and questions about the campaign or land conservation are easily transmitted, improving the campaign's understanding of voters' concerns.

· Fundraisers can take all of their off-line activities on-line, including event registration, direct contributions, communications with donors, and so on. The site itself may not attract many new, unsolicited donors, but it can make giving by existing donors more convenient and can provide an effective way for the campaign to track these contributors. Be sure to check with your state and local campaign finance office before soliciting or accepting campaign contributions electronically.

· A web site may aid in organizing and get-out-the-vote efforts, such as facilitating absentee ballot requests, recruiting volunteers, and providing polling locations. Email has also become an important tool for increasing and maintaining communications with supporters. An understanding of the tools to manage supporter databases is essential. More sophisticated campaigns can track volunteers with on-line databases, even assigning at-home tasks via email. Your volunteers, for instance, can download the campaign's message points and send letters to the editor.

The costs of a professionally designed web site can vary widely: local races may be able to get the site designed pro bono or utilize a one-size-fits-all template for roughly $1,000, with additional cost for hosting and maintenance; sites for large

---

THE INTERNET REMAINS AS ONE OF THE CHEAPEST AND EASIEST WAYS TO COMMUNICATE WITH CONSTITUENTS AND POTENTIAL SUPPORTERS. IT DOESN'T REPLACE TELEVISION ADVERTISING, DIRECT MAIL, OR A GOOD ARTICLE IN A NEWSPAPER, BUT A STRONG WEB SITE AND INTERNET STRATEGY CAN BE AN INVALUABLE TOOL FOR DISTRIBUTING INFORMATION WIDELY AND WISELY.

BRIAN REICH
ELECTIONMOUSE.COM

statewide races may cost between $15,000 and $25,000. Whatever the budget, Internet campaign strategist Phil Nash of Campaign Advantage recommends that you spend enough on a hosting company (going price is $40 per month) to

---

Welcome!

Check out our ever growing list of individual and organizational ENDORSEMENTS!

Dear Neighbor,

You are invited to join friends, family and neighbors to support the VOTE YES ON 1 campaign. This past spring the Dakota County board of Commissioners authored a common sense levy referendum to protect water quality, farmland and natural areas. We want you to join us!

This web page as well as other materials disseminated through out the campaign will be an opportunity to learn more about the County Question 1 referendum and reasons to support it.

Please join your neighbors, friends and family who are working to protect natural areas and farmland and who believe our successful efforts will enhance water quality for all of Dakota County, now and for future generations. We ask for your support and participation for our unique natural treasures and agricultural heritage in Dakota County

To support the campaign please contact Michael Quest at Dakota Citizens for Land and Water, 651-287-0683 or email at msquest@bitstream.net.

Sincerely,

Rick Hanson   **Beverly Topps, Co-Chair**

SOURCE: DAKOTA CITIZENS FOR LAND AND WATER, A PROJECT OF THE CONSERVATION CAMPAIGN.

THE WEB SITE FROM A SUCCESSFUL CONSERVATION MEASURE IN DAKOTA COUNTY, MINNESOTA, HELPED PROVIDE INFORMATION AND KEY MESSAGES ABOUT THE CAMPAIGN. IT ALSO ENCOURAGED SUPPORTERS TO HELP AND CONTRIBUTE. THIS LETTER WELCOMED VISITORS TO THE WEB SITE.

ensure responsiveness, and reserve half of your overall
Internet campaign budget for site maintenance and
email campaigning.[34]

If you decide to create a campaign web site, keep it simple
and stay on message. Make the site easy to find, selecting a
domain name that reflects the measure's name or message.
Keep the site updated, even daily. Make sure it gives people a
way to contact you by email and phone. Integrate your web site
with other campaign activities, complementing media, field
efforts, and fundraising. And finally, design your site with
different audiences in mind: the press, undecided voters,
supporters, and potential contributors.

SETTING UP YOUR FIELD ORGANIZATION

Almost no campaign has the time and resources to contact and
discuss the issues with every registered voter. In fact, you'll likely
contact very few. Ten percent—say, 2,500 people in a town with
25,000 registered voters—is a solid effort. Yet even a limited
field program—if it is well planned and well executed—can make
the difference on election day.

The fact is, most local land conservation elections are either
low turnout (for example, a special election) or low profile
(receiving little attention during a presidential or gubernatorial
election), or both. Having a voter hear your conservation message
from a neighbor or a volunteer phoner can be indispensable.

Times have changed: caller ID and unlisted numbers create
new challenges for a phone operation, and the prevalence of
telemarketers and solicitors has resulted in a more wary and
suspicious public. Yet grassroots campaigning is still an incred-
ibly valuable tool. Direct voter contact is like no other, because it

has the authenticity of a credible source and a personal message. Through your field program you meet voters where they live, give a human face to an issue, and allow voters the opportunity to ask questions.

So how do you spend limited field resources—financial and volunteer—in the most effective way? There are several important factors to consider. First, you must determine how many voters the campaign can contact. That means taking a close look at the strength and depth of your volunteers (and/or paid field resources).

Next, you must determine which groups of voters the campaign should phone or visit first. Your polling and targeting analysis have helped define the campaign's targeted universe. But beyond that, there are several more practical considerations such as the accessibility of neighborhoods (consider steep grades, remote areas, apartment buildings, and so on) and the number of listed phone numbers.

Finally, you must decide how to focus your resources. Is the highest priority to persuade likely voters to support your measure or to increase turnout among less likely voters who are predisposed to support your measure? You may have found through polling that certain voters (perhaps Latinos, women under age 40, or a certain council district) are heavily in favor of your measure. There is an opportunity through the field program to increase turnout among such targeted groups. Phoning can help you reach targeted groups of voters who are not geographically based and too difficult to reach through a walk program.

With regular voters, use the field program to get your messages out and persuade them to vote your way. Especially if you don't have the resources to do much paid media, your volunteer, grassroots field program can make a difference.

THE PRECINCT CAPTAIN

Precinct captains have their roots in the big-city ward bosses of years ago. As part of the party machine, these individuals helped bring services to a neighborhood, kept political leaders abreast of local needs and developments, and organized and got-out-the-vote on election day. Take away the graft and corruption and you have the essence of a good precinct captain today: someone who knows the neighborhood, can speak to the issues, and motivates the community. Precinct captains are the heart of a field operation, helping organize a neighborhood, contacting voters door to door or by phone, enlisting volunteers, and distributing lawn signs. They are also the eyes and ears of the campaign, spreading the campaign's message at the grass-roots level and reporting back about voters' concerns.

Larger, well-funded campaigns will have the resources to hire field organizers. These organizers can enlist precinct captains and other volunteers. A low-budget campaign may rely entirely on volunteers, and precinct captains can assume responsibility for organizing a neighborhood. In most cases precinct captains will be given a specially targeted voter list (most often in their own neighborhood) and encouraged to contact as many people on the list as possible by walking door to door or phoning. With a precinct-by-precinct voter analysis, you can give the precinct captain your target number. Whether you hope to win by 100 votes or minimize your losses by 50, these goals can be important motivators. Precinct captains should be given talking points for the key messages but should also be encouraged to speak personally about the importance of the measure to their neighborhood.

Most precincts are manageable, either by the captain alone or with the help of volunteers he or she recruits. The key is to find dedicated, responsible precinct captains. Where do you find them? Your own volunteer base is the best place to start. Many campaigns get a lot of genuine offers of help. These people need to be managed, trained, and put to work. Beyond that, tap local environmental activists, tried-and-true precinct captains from the campaigns of supportive elected officials, and members of organizations that support the measure.

Your volunteer coordinator, field director, or campaign manager should clearly outline the responsibilities of a precinct captain and give this written list to anyone who agrees to take the job. Tasks can include identifying supporters door to door or by phone, distributing literature, arranging neighborhood coffees, selling tickets to a fundraiser, putting up yard signs, and getting out the vote on election day. Make sure the precinct captain is willing and able to perform all the duties on the list. If there is something she or he doesn't want to do, try to line up another volunteer to fill in the gaps. The volunteer coordinator should keep a list of all the tasks assigned to each precinct captain and regularly check to make sure progress is being made. In turn, campaign managers need to remember to listen to the suggestions of a precinct captain. They know the people and the neighborhood.

In addition to a list of duties, prepare a volunteer packet. This packet can contain a street map of the precinct, a list of registered voters (with appropriate codes to mark supporters, opponents, undecided voters, potential volunteers, and voters willing to take yard signs), campaign literature, instruction sheets for phoning and going door to door, scheduling forums for coffees, and absentee ballot applications. If you decide to use them, give the precinct captain some yard signs (but not too many; you don't want them to sit in the trunk of someone's car).

WALKING DOOR TO DOOR

Volunteer walkers can help contact voters in precincts with no precinct captains, or they can assist the precinct captains in larger neighborhoods. One effective way to organize precinct captains and other volunteer walkers (and phoners) is through a weekend rally or walk kickoff. Volunteers can meet in the morning to share news and information about the campaign, perhaps hear a pep talk by a public official, enjoy coffee and doughnuts, and receive campaign messages and field instructions. Walkers are charged with going door to door, passing out a brochure about the campaign, and talking with voters about the measure. Voters are recorded as supporters, opponents, or undecideds. Supporters can be asked to volunteer, post a lawn sign, or sign an endorsement card. It is recommended that people walk in teams of two, one on each side of the street. This teamwork makes walking timely and safe. If voters are not home, volunteers should drop off the literature with a handwritten "sorry I missed you" message at the door.

Some other commonsense tips for walking: make sure volunteers are dressed appropriately and are presentable, remind them of the importance of courtesy, instruct them to stick to the pitch and gauge the voter's interest level before overwhelming them with information, and record the name of every voter appropriately. Also consider providing volunteers with name badges. These can give walkers credibility and communicate the campaign's name and message.

You will probably want to modify your walk lists to print odd numbers of the streets on one sheet and even numbers on the other. You may also want to exclude from your walk lists low-propensity voters, or voters from certain demographic groups that research shows are strongly opposed to your measure.

VOLUNTEER PHONE BANKING

Theoretically, if you have a strong precinct captain in every precinct you may not need to do much phoning before the election day get-out-the-vote effort. But chances are that there will be targeted precincts without precinct captains, large precincts that cannot be completed in time, and hard-to-walk precincts that are best reached by phone. Here's where a volunteer phone bank can be critical.

Before you begin a phone bank, assess how many calls your volunteers can make. A "contact" means actually getting the voter on the other end of the phone; it does not mean leaving a message, getting a busy signal and moving on, or getting a wrong number. Depending on your community, the accuracy of your list, and the strength of your volunteers, you can expect between five and fifteen contacts per hour per person. Use these estimates to determine the number of contacts you can make during a phone bank, over a week of phoning, and for the length of the campaign.

Phones, voter lists, scripts, tally sheets, and motivated volunteers are the ingredients of a successful phone bank. If

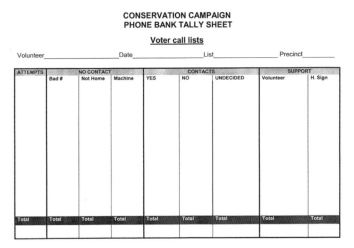

**CONSERVATION CAMPAIGN
PHONE BANK TALLY SHEET**

<u>**Voter call lists**</u>

Volunteer_____ Date_____ List_____ Precinct_____

ATTEMPTS	NO CONTACT			CONTACTS			SUPPORT	
	Bad #	Not Home	Machine	YES	NO	UNDECIDED	Volunteer	H. Sign
Total	Total	Total	Total	Total	Total	Total	Total	Total

A TALLY SHEET CAN HELP A CAMPAIGN TRACK THE OVERALL PROGRESS OF ITS PHONE BANK OPERATION.

you have no campaign headquarters or your headquarters does not have many phones, try to borrow office space in the evenings and on weekends from a friendly business or law office with ample phones. The list vendor you used for your direct mailing can also provide you with phone lists. These lists will contain voter names, phone numbers, and codes to mark supporters (YES), opponents (NO), undecideds (U.D.), and voters who have agreed to volunteer and/or post a yard sign.

Round up a team of volunteers to call for several hours at a time into targeted precincts. The best times to call are during the week between 6:00 P.M. and 9:00 P.M. and weekends between 9:00 A.M. and 9:00 P.M. (You're probably less likely to catch people at home on Friday and Saturday nights.) If you have volunteers available weekdays, try having them call into precincts with large numbers of senior citizens who are more apt to be reachable during the day.

Train your volunteers well before they pick up the phone, by explaining to them the importance of phoning to the campaign, and preparing them for unwelcoming voters, hang-ups, and so on. Give them a script to follow and background information about the measure and the campaign. Above all, if they don't know the answer to a voter's question, make sure they are willing to find out and call back (or have someone from the campaign call back).

Depending on the campaign strategy, the calls will be either persuasion or identification calls. Voter identification calls are fairly quick and easy, designed simply to determine the voter's intent on the measure in question for use in a future get-out-the-vote effort. Persuasion calls are designed to convey information about the measure in the hopes of picking up new votes. You should determine the number of supporters you want to identify and get to the polls on election day. Based on poll results (the threshold question) you can estimate how many

CONSERVATION FINANCE HANDBOOK

calls must be made to reach your goal. For instance, say you want to identify 1,500 supporters. If your poll shows that 60 percent of likely voters support your measure, then you'll need names and phone numbers for 900 voters. But phone numbers are not 100 percent accurate and you usually can't reach all voters with numbers. Expect a drop-off rate of 10 to 20 percent. That means that you'll need 90 to 180 extra names and phone numbers to reach your target.

You'll want to begin calling about four to six weeks before election day. Be sure to end your calling in enough time to process the data and prepare for election day get-out-the-vote—a couple of days to a week out.

VOTING BY MAIL

A vote-by-mail ballot program can be an important part of a field program. By identifying supporters and encouraging them to vote absentee, you have votes in your column before election day.

Vote-by-mail laws vary from state to state. On one end of the spectrum are states that require voters to register for absentee ballots at each election and state the reason for the request. At the other end are states that allow for permanent absentee voting to anyone who wants it. Carefully research the regulations in your state governing absentee and early voting.

If it is allowed, begin by encouraging supporters to vote by mail. When a supporter is identified through the field program, offer an absentee ballot application (by mail or at the door) and explain the importance of voting by mail. Once they are registered to vote absentee, track these voters through the elections office to make sure they've returned their ballots. Follow up whenever necessary by phone and at the door. Make sure to follow the rules for absentee ballot application procedures exactly, including the deadlines for returning applications, signature requirements, and whether the application must be returned by the applicant or can be picked up by the campaign and returned.

In some places, voters are allowed to cast their votes in the days or weeks before the election at a designated polling place. If your state allows for early voting, be sure to incorporate this into your field program. Encourage early voting by providing supporters with information about the process and assistance to the polls.

ORGANIZING NEIGHBORHOOD COFFEES AND HOUSE PARTIES

Imagine that you're invited next door for coffee and dessert. A group of your neighbors meet in the living room to discuss the upcoming election. On the ballot: a measure that will protect threatened land and your community's quality of life. A knowledgeable campaign volunteer explains the details of the measure, provides literature, and answers questions. You agree to support the measure, post a sign on your front lawn, and even make a small contribution to the campaign. What better way to inform people and get them involved?

Neighborhood coffees or house parties provide a relaxed, friendly forum for reaching voters. When neighbor invites neighbor, you have a willing, attentive audience. Use these events to increase voter awareness of your measure, and to identify supporters, volunteers, and donors.

These events are, however, time consuming to organize, and they probably won't reach all the swing voters in a given neighborhood. Have precinct captains organize them in targeted neighborhoods. Campaign staff, precinct captains, and/or surrogate speakers can attend the events and brief the participants. Make sure that follow-up, including written thank-you notes and answers to questions, is done quickly. (Refer to page 136 to learn how to use house parties for fundraising.)

SAMPLE PHONE SCRIPTS

AUDIENCE: Likely voters

PURPOSE: Persuasion

SCRIPT: Hi, my name is [name of caller] from the Land and Water Protection Committee. Is [name of voter] home?

I'm calling to urge you to vote YES on a land purchase bond that will be on the ballot November 2nd. This measure will protect land around watersheds and streams that keeps our drinking water clean and prevents flooding. All expenditures will be subject to an annual independent audit and review by a citizens advisory committee. This measure has been endorsed by the chamber of commerce and the free press because it ensures fiscal accountability and protects our land and water resources. Can we count on your support, or would you like more information about the measure?

IF IN SUPPORT: Thanks for your support and don't forget that Tuesday, November 2nd, is election day.

WANTS MORE INFORMATION: I'll be mailing you a package of materials about the bond. And please feel free to contact me at the number listed if you have any questions.

IF OPPOSED: Thanks for your time.

AUDIENCE: Likely voters

PURPOSE: Identify supporters. This group will later be targeted in get-out-the-vote activities such as a follow-up phone call.

SCRIPT: Is [name of voter] there? Hi, my name is [name of caller] and I'm a volunteer with the YES on D campaign. We're conducting a brief survey of voters in your community about the upcoming November 5th election.

The measure on the ballot asks voters if they will support a $50 million parks and recreation bond. Specifically, the bonds will pay for the acquisition of land for open spaces, natural areas, and environmental enhancements and for renovation and safety improvements at recreational facilities and playgrounds.

If the election were held today, do you think you'd vote YES or NO on the measure?

IF YES: Is that definitely or probably YES? Thank you for your time. (Eliminate probably YES voters from the final tally of supporters.)

IF NO: Thank you for your time. (Eliminate from the final list.)

IF NOT SURE: Thank you for your time. (Eliminate from the final list.)

AUDIENCE: Identified supporters

PURPOSE: Get-out-the-vote

SCRIPT: Hello, may I speak with [name of voter]? My name is [name of caller] and I'm calling on behalf of the Open Space and Clean Water Committee to urge you to vote YES on Proposition 4 this Tuesday. We need your support to preserve Jackson County's land and water resources before they're lost to development. This measure will protect the land that helps keep our drinking water safe and our air clean for our families and future generations.

Tomorrow is election day. We urge you to vote YES on Proposition 4. Thank you.

IF ANSWERING MACHINE: Leave message on machine.

ORGANIZING A SPEAKERS BUREAU

Supporters of the $40 million land conservation bond in Beaufort County, North Carolina, credit an aggressive speakers bureau for much of the measure's success. In less than six weeks, the campaign reached out to 65 groups, communicating facts about the measure and the campaign's message.

Public forums in which to communicate the campaign's message will probably be far too numerous for the campaign manager to attend them all. That's where a speakers bureau comes in. A speakers bureau is an organized group of volunteers who can speak effectively and persuasively about the measure at community and political meetings large and small, presenting information about the measure and answering questions.

Of course, it is ideal to recruit experienced public speakers, but if you have volunteers with strong potential and little public speaking experience, consider training them. Recruit a variety of supporters to serve on the speakers bureau. That way you'll be able to match the most appropriate volunteer to the audience. Volunteers can include political leaders, community activists, business leaders, and even college students. As much as possible, look for a link between the volunteer speaker and the organization hosting the forum—membership with the group, an understanding of their issues, or a close relationship to the community, for example. And be sure that the volunteer speaker is well briefed about the measure and the event. The speaker must understand the basic facts about the measure, the campaign's key messages, and some background about the organization sponsoring the event.

THE NUTS AND BOLTS OF TRACKING VOTERS

You have lined up precinct captains in targeted precincts. Callers man the phones several nights a week. You're organizing volunteers to get-out-the-vote on election day. Now tracking their work and managing all that new data become more important than ever.

Through the phone and walk programs (whether you're in identification or persuasion mode), voters will be marked as supporters, opponents, or undecideds. Codes should also include "not home" (walkers), "no answer" (phoners), and "wrong number or disconnected" (phoners).

While "no" voters will be disregarded, more needs to be done with undecideds and supporters. For instance, supporters may also be classified as potential volunteers, recipients of lawn signs, or included on endorsement lists. And undecideds can be contacted again in any number of ways. Once a phoner has completed his calls at the end of the night, for example, he can be responsible for mailing out a form letter (with a personal note on a Post-it note, perhaps) to all supporters and undecideds on his list. The letter can simply say, "Good to talk to you about the open space protection measure, thanks for your support," or

"Hope you consider supporting this important issue on election day and here's some more information."

All this information needs to be tracked and managed, culminating with reliable data that can be used for get-out-the-vote. Assuming that your campaign is tracking more than a few hundred voters, you'll need at least one personal computer and a person knowledgeable in database programs. Try to get a computer and printer loaned or donated. And if your campaign is large enough to warrant it, get a more basic model for general campaign use and a better one for the person in charge of data management. Your computers will be invaluable to your field operation—and necessary to write letters, print labels, and generate lists for the entire campaign.

Your database will include lists of voters contacted through the field program as well as media lists, contributors, precinct captains,

PRECINCT # 0002301		RES CITY	CLARKVILLE		PHONE LIST	1/24/2004
ADDR.	NAME	G A R	PHONE	-VOTER TAG-	AFF/COMMENTS	
2 MAIN ST	MATTHEW G ALEXANDER	M 38 D	000-0000	NH Y N U LS		
4 MAIN ST	LEIGH WRIGHT	F 56 D	000-0000	NH Y N U LS		
6 MAIN ST	SHIRLEY B ANDERSON	F 81 D	664-0222	NH Y N U LS		
6 MAIN ST	DONALD B ANDERSON	M 88 D	664-0222	NH Y N U LS		
8 MAIN ST	CHARLOTTE L MAITLAND	F 41 D	795-7944	NH Y N U LS		
10 MAIN ST	CHRISTINE A GUGLIELMETTI	F 39 R	000-0000	NH Y N U LS		
12 MAIN ST	PAUL J WILSON	M 38 R	664-8771	NH Y N U LS		
12 MAIN ST	SANDRA MARIE WILSON	F 38 R	664-8771	NH Y N U LS		
14 MAIN ST	KATHLEEN C DOUGAN	F 55 R	000-0000	NH Y N U LS		
16 MAIN ST	PATRICIA A BATHURST	F 35 R	795-6735	NH Y N U LS		
16 MAIN ST	HENRY M MURPHY	M 53 R	000-0000	NH Y N U LS		
16 MAIN ST	SUSAN A MURPHY	F 51 R	000-0000	NH Y N U LS		
20 MAIN ST	DEBORAH D HAHN	F 50 D	795-7341	NH Y N U LS		
22 MAIN ST	JACKSON D BIRD	M 21 I	792-1437	NH Y N U LS		
22 MAIN ST	OLIVIA L MARTINEZ	F 58 D	792-1437	NH Y N U LS		

A VOTER LIST CONTAINS VOTER NAME, ADDRESS, PHONE NUMBER (IF AVAILABLE), VOTE HISTORY, AND CODES TO TRACK HIS OR HER POSITION ON THE ISSUE. NH=NOT HOME; Y=YES; N=NO; U=UNDECIDED; LS=LAWN SIGN. BAR CODES ON THE FAR RIGHT ARE USED TO ENTER VOTER INFORMATION INTO A CAMPAIGN'S DATABASE.

and volunteers. The field program lists will include subsets of voters such as lawn sign recipients. Further, some lists obtained through government election offices may not come in the form you need (as opposed to lists purchased through voter file vendors, which can be modified to your specifications). Your computer consultant may need to adapt the lists to include only the relevant information, such as names, phone numbers, and codes.

Once the data from the field program have been gathered, take a couple of days to assemble the information for get-out-the-vote. That means producing final voter lists of identified supporters, by precinct, for volunteers to contact by phone or on foot on election day and the day prior.

GETTING-OUT-THE-VOTE

The primary objective of your field program may have been to identify supporters and increase turnout on election day. Or you may have been persuading undecided likely voters to support your measure. In either case, you must make every effort to identify these voters and get them to the polls on election day.

Your get-out-the-vote activities begin well before election day. Consider all the tools you can use to help get-out-your-vote, including communications through direct mail, radio, and yard signs. Then go to work preparing your field program for get-out-the-vote activities, assembling data, preparing lists, and reconfirming volunteers.

For get-out-the-vote on election day, determine which neighborhoods are best contacted by phone and which can be walked. Phoning can begin the Monday before election day, with an election day reminder, a message about the measure, and a "thanks for your support" message. These calls can be made by volunteers, or you can work with a firm that specializes in paid phoning.

Walkers can also hit the streets on Monday evening, preferably hanging door hangers with an election day reminder and campaign message. Election day walking can begin bright and early, with precinct captains and other volunteers meeting at the headquarters in the morning. Here's the basic election day drill:

- Precinct captains, walkers, and phoners meet at the headquarters and are given election day instructions, supporter lists, and a pep talk.

- At midday, precinct captains and walkers go to polling places to check voters lists. Supporters on their lists who have voted are crossed off.

- Walkers visit supporters on the list who haven't yet voted to encourage the voter to go to the poll, or leave a second door hanger. They can offer rides and assistance to voters who need it.

- In the late afternoon, phoners arrive to call into precincts that are not being walked, or phoners can complete a precinct begun by a walker. Ideally, phoners get their list, go to the polling place to check off people who have voted, and return to call through the list.

- The process continues until the polls close.

Absentee and early voters should also be tracked in the weeks leading up to election day. Check with the elections office regularly to track voters, encouraging supporters to cast their vote.

AFTER ELECTION DAY

When the work is done and the polls have closed, have a party and wait for returns. This is a good opportunity to thank supporters, volunteers, public officials, contributors, and endorsers. Invite the press to cover the event and line up the most appropriate spokespeople to comment on the results.

When the celebration is over, it is time to close out the campaign accounts and file final reports. Be sure that all the books are in order and that the paperwork is completed properly and promptly. Check with your legal counsel, if available. Successful conservation financing is often a long-term pursuit involving an investment of time, money, strategy, and coalition building over several years.

If you lose, carefully evaluate why. Bring key players together to assess strengths and weaknesses of the measure and the campaign, regroup, and consider another try.

Several campaigns have had better luck the second time around. After experiencing the largest building boom in its history during the 1980s, Cape Cod residents seemed eager to protect the region's wetlands, wildlife habitat, and other natural areas. Yet the next decade was marked by bitter disputes about how to fund conservation, pitting Realtors against conservationists and community activists. In January 1998, Cape Cod voters defeated a conservation land bank proposal that would have increased the real-estate transfer tax—a measure actively opposed by the Realtors association. Low voter turnout at the special election enabled the opposition to influence the outcome with heavy spending that brought a disproportionate number of opponents to the polls.

After the defeat, both sides joined forces to help craft a new proposal. The resulting measure called for land banks funded in each town with a 3 percent property tax surcharge. An unusual

coalition of Realtors, environmentalists, and legislators shepherded the second proposal through the state legislature and
onto the ballot for a town-by-town vote in November 1998.
All 15 towns approved the new land bank decisively in a high-
turnout, general election.

Conservation proponents in Adams County, Colorado, also
came back from defeat. In 1997, voters rejected a measure to
raise the sales tax for open space protection. Two years later, a
second conservation sales tax measure passed by a 60 percent
margin. This winning measure was designed to reflect voters'
conservation priorities and fiscal concerns.

Clearly circumstances change and proponents learn. If you
decide to try again, be strategic, be smart, and focus on what you
can do to conserve the land in your community. ∎

Endnotes

1. *LandVote, Americans Invest in Parks & Open Space* (Boston, Washington, D.C.: The Trust for Public Land and the Land Trust Alliance, 2002), p. 1.

2. Will Rogers, The Trust for Public Land, remarks at the Green Space Design Conference, Park City, Utah, March 1, 2001.

3. Linda E. Hollis and William Fulton, *Open Space Protection: Conservation Meets Growth Management* (Washington, D.C.: The Brookings Institution on Urban and Metropolitan Growth, April 2002), pp. vi, 6.

4. Steve Lerner and William Poole, *The Economic Benefits of Parks and Open Space* (San Francisco: The Trust for Public Land, 1999), p. 8.

5. John L. Crompton, Lisa L. Love, and Thomas A. More, "An Empirical Study of the Role of Recreation, Parks, and Open Space in Companies' (Re) Location Decisions," *Journal of Park and Recreation Administration* (1997): pp. 37–58.

6. D. Ernest Cook and William P. Ryan, *Community Open Space: New Techniques for Acquisition and Financing*, MIS Report (Washington, D.C.: The International City/County Management Association, 1993), p. 2.

7. "Jacksonville, Florida: Guiding Metropolitan Growth," The Trust for Public Land, www.tpl.org , 1999.

8. Hollis and Fulton, *Open Space Protection*, pp. 25–26.

9. John L. Crompton, *Financing and Acquiring Park and Recreation Resources* (Champaign, Ill.: Human Kinetics Publishers, 1999), pp. 477–480.

10. Julie Freedgood and Edward Thompson, Jr., *Saving American Farmland: What Works* (Washington, D.C.: American Farmland Trust, 1997), p. 36.

11. LandVote, *Americans Invest in Parks & Open Space*.

12. Steven Glazer, quoted in ibid., pp. 16–17.

13. Phyllis Myers, *GreenSense* (San Francisco: The Trust for Public Land, spring 1997).

14. Esther Feldman, "The Proposition A Story: How Los Angeles County Voters Gained $540 Million for Parks, Recreation, and Natural Lands," *Local Open Space Financing Campaigns* (San Francisco: The Trust for Public Land, 1994), pp. 13, 37.

15. Mark Mellman and Michael Bloomfield, "How to Pick a Consultant: Hiring Pollsters," *Campaign & Elections* (July 2001), p. 4.

16. Corey Brown, "Public Opinion Polling: Your Road Map to Success," *Local Open Space Financing Campaigns: A Handbook of Case Studies* (San Francisco: The Trust for Public Land, 1994), p. 2.

17. Ibid., pp. 3–5.

18. Corey Brown, quoted in ibid., p. 3.

19. American Statistical Association, *What Are Focus Groups?*, 1997, p. 1.

20. Frank Luntz, *The Polling Report*, May 16 and 20, 1994, p. 6.

21. Focus groups conducted by Doak, Carrier, and O'Donnell, Washington, D.C.

22. Peter G. Sortino, phone interview by author, August 2002.

23. Cook and Ryan, "Community Open Space," p. 5.

24. Brown, "Public Opinion Polling," p. 9.

25. World Wildlife Fund, "Local Land Acquisition for Conservation: Trends and Factors to Consider," reproduced in *Local Open Space Financing Campaigns*, p. 19.

26. Ibid., pp. 18–20.

27. S. J. Guzzetta, *The Campaign Manual: A Definitive Study of the Modern Political Process*, 5th ed. (Alexandria, Va.: Political Publications, www.americangotv.com, 2000), p. 155.

28. Catherine Shaw, *The Campaign Manager: Running and Winning Local Elections* (Boulder, Colo.: Westview Press, 2000), p. 3.

29. Thomas R. Asher, *Foundations and Ballot Measures: A Legal Guide* (Washington, D.C.: The Alliance for Justice, 1998), p. 8.

30. Russell Shay, LandVote, *Americans Invest in Parks & Open Space*, p. 2.

31. Judge Lawrence Grey, *How to Win a Local Election: The Guide to Organizing Your Campaign* (New York: M. Evans & Company, 1999), p. 179.

32. Ann Beaudry and Bob Schaeffer, *Winning Local and State Elections: The Guide to Organizing Your Campaign* (New York: The Free Press, 1986), p. 167.

33. Becky Donatelli, "Consultant Q&A: Campaigning on the Internet," *Campaigns & Elections* (September 2002), p. 60.

34. Phil Nash, "Consultant Q&A: Campaigning on the Internet" *Campaigns & Elections* (September 2002), p. 53.

Bibliography and Resources

CAMPAIGN RESOURCES

The Campaign Manager, 2nd edition. Catherine Shaw. Boulder, Colo.: Westview Press, 2000. This book is about running and winning local elections.

The Campaign Manual, 5th edition. Alexandria, Va.: Political Publications, 2000. This book is a definitive study of the modern political campaign process.

Foundations and Ballot Measures: A Legal Guide. Thomas R. Asher. Washington, D.C.: The Alliance for Justice, 1998. This book complements *Seize the Initiative*, explaining the role of foundations in ballot measure campaigns.

How to Run for Local Office. Robert J. Thomas. Westland, Mich.: RT Enterprises, 1999. This is a complete guide for winning a local election.

How to Win a Local Election: The Guide to Organizing Your Campaign. Judge Lawrence Grey. New York: M. Evans & Company, 1999. This is a step-by-step guide to running a local campaign.

LandVote. Boston, Washington, D.C.: The Trust for Public Land and the Land Trust Alliance, published annually. LandVote provides the nation's most comprehensive accounting of state and local ballot measures for parks and open space funding. Complete *LandVote* reports are available at www.tpl.org.

Local Open Space Financing Campaigns: A Handbook of TPL Case Studies. Ernest Cook, editor. Boston, Mass.: The Trust for Public Land, 1994. This handbook provides articles about and case studies of local conservation campaigns across the country.

Political Resource Directory. Carol Hess, editor. Washington, D.C.: Political Resources, annual publication. This comprehensive guide lists professional organizations that provide services and products for the political community. It includes the official directory for the American Association of Political Consultants.

Seize the Initiative. Gregory L. Colvin and Lowell Finely. Washington, D.C.: The Alliance for Justice, 1996. This book explains to nonprofit organizations the legal do's and don'ts of working on ballot measure campaigns.

Winning Local & State Elections: The Guide to Organizing Your Campaign. Ann Beaudry and Bob Schaeffer. New York: The Free Press, 1986. This is a comprehensive book about campaign strategy and organization.

LAND CONSERVATION RESOURCES

Building Green Infrastructure: Land Conservation as Water Protection Strategy. San Francisco: The Trust for Public Land, 1999. This report presents the cases of four watersheds where land conservation is helping preserve water quality. For a copy of the report, contact TPL at (415) 495-4014 or www.tpl.org.

Doing Deals: A Guide to Buying Land for Conservation. San Francisco: The Trust for Public Land and the Land Trust Alliance, 1995. This book introduces basic real-estate, financial, and strategic principles at work in the world of conservation real estate. For a copy of the book, contact the Land Trust Alliance at (202) 638-4725 or www.lta.org/publication/.

The Economic Benefits of Parks and Open Space: How Land Conservation Helps Communities Grow Smart and Protect the Bottom Line. Steven Lerner and William Poole. San Francisco: The Trust for Public Land, 1999. This report offers ample evidence that open space protection is a wise investment with important economic benefits, attracting investment, revitalizing cities, boosting tourism, protecting farms and ranches, preventing flood damage, and safeguarding the environment. For a copy of the report, contact TPL at (415) 495-4014 or www.tpl.org.

Getting to Smart Growth: 100 Policies for Implementation. Washington, D.C.: Smart Growth Network and International City/County Managers Association. This is the fourth primer in a series on the benefits and techniques of smart growth. This report aims to support communities that have recognized the value and importance of smart growth and now seek to implement it. The report is available at www.smartgrowth.org.

Green Infrastructure: Smart Conservation for the 21st Century.
Mark A. Benedict, Ph.D., and Edward T. McMahon.
Washington, D.C.: Sprawl Watch Clearinghouse, 2001.
This report discusses the protection of green infrastructure
as part of a community's smart-growth efforts. For a copy of
the report, contact the Sprawl Watch Clearinghouse at
www.sprawlwatch.org or The Conservation Fund at
www.conservationfund.org.

*The Impact of Parks and Open Space and Property Values and the
Property Tax Base.* John L. Crompton, Ph.D. College Station,
Tex.: Texas A&M University, 2000. This report examines the
economic contributions of parks and open space through their
impact on property values. For a copy of the report, visit the
Texas A&M web site at www.rpts.tamu.edu.

*Local Greenprinting for Growth: Using Land Conservation to Guide
Growth and Preserve the Character of Communities.* San Francisco:
The Trust for Public Land and the National Association of
Counties, 2003. This report series is designed to help local
officials design and implement a conservation vision to protect
a community's most important land and water resources.
For a copy of the reports, contact TPL at (415) 495-4014
or www.tpl.org.

*Local Parks, Local Financing, Volume I: Increasing Public Investment in
Parks & Open Space.* Kim Hopper. San Francisco: The Trust for
Public Land, 1999. This report outlines the various tools for
raising conservation funds at the local level. For a copy of the
report, contact TPL at (415) 495-4014 or www.tpl.org.

Local Parks, Local Financing, Volume II: Paying for Urban Parks Without Raising Taxes. Peter Harnik. San Francisco: The Trust for Public Land, 1999. This report provides information about non-tax funding of urban parks and recreation programs. For a copy of the report, contact TPL at (415) 495-4014 or www.tpl.org.

Open Space Protection: Conservation Meets Growth Management. Linda W. Hollis, AICP, and William Fulton. Washington, D.C.: The Brookings Institution, 2002. This report provides an overview of the nature, quantity, and objectives of open space programs in the United States and describes how they affect the shape and form of metropolitan areas. For a copy of the report, contact the Brookings Institution at www.brookings.edu.

Saving American Farmland: What Works. Julia Freedgood. Washington, D.C.: American Farmland Trust, 1997. This comprehensive guidebook presents the American Farmland Trust's latest research on farmland protection. Specifically designed for policy makers, planners, community organizations, and concerned citizens who are working to save farmland at the local level, Saving American Farmland discusses the challenges of farming on the edge of development and illustrates the value of farmland to our nation, states, and communities. To order this book, contact the American Farmland Trust at (413) 586-9330 or www.farmland.org.

THE
TRUST
for
PUBLIC
LAND

About
The Trust for Public Land

The Trust for Public Land conserves land for people to enjoy as parks, gardens, and other natural places, ensuring livable communities for generations to come.

Experts in community building, real estate, finance, conservation, and politics help communities through all stages of the conservation process, including:

· Creating a conservation vision by protecting important land that may be threatened by urban or suburban sprawl

· Pioneering new ways to finance parks and open space and promoting the importance of public lands

· Working with landowners, government agencies, and community groups to acquire and manage land

TPL believes that connecting people to land will deepen the public's appreciation of nature and the commitment to protect it. Since 1972, TPL has helped protect more than 1.5 million acres in 46 states—expansive recreation areas, historic homesteads, pocket-sized city parks, working landscapes, and urban gardens.

TPL's Conservation Finance Program helps communities, states, lands trusts, and others create and expand public funding for land conservation. Learn more at www.tpl.org.

TPL'S CONSERVATION FINANCE TEAM

Ernest Cook, Director
33 Union St., 5th Floor
Boston, MA 02108
(617) 367-6200

Adam Eichberg,
Associate Director—West
Conservation Finance Program
(303) 837-1414

Will Abberger,
Associate Director—East
Conservation Finance Program
(850) 222-7911 x23

Bill Johnston,
Executive Director
The Conservation Campaign
(202) 543-6102

NATIONAL RESOURCES FOR OPEN SPACE PROTECTION

American Farmland Trust
(202) 331-7300
www.farmland.org

The Conservation Fund
(703) 525-6300
www.conservationfund.org

Ducks Unlimited
(202) 347-1530
www.ducks.org

Environmental Protection Agency
(202) 260-2750
www.epa.gov/smartgrowth

Land Trust Alliance
(202) 638-4725
www.lta.org

National Recreation and
   Park Association
(703) 858-0784
www.nrpa.org

National Trust for
Historic Preservation
(202) 588-6000
www.nthp.org

The Nature Conservancy
(800) 628-6860
www.nature.org

Rails-to-Trails Conservancy
(202) 331-9696
www.railtrails.org

The Trust for Public Land
(415) 495-4014
(202) 543-7552
www.tpl.org

U.S. Forest Service
(202) 205-8333
www.fs.fed.us

CONSERVATION FINANCE HANDBOOK

Index

501(c)(3), 18, 101, 104–105, 107
501(c)(4), IX, 101, 105, 107, 130
Absentee ballot. *See* field
Acquiring and managing the land, 6
Acquisition methods, 74–75, 79
Adams County, Colorado, 92, 186
Administrative costs. *See* fiscal safeguards
Advertising. *See* paid media
Advisory committees. *See* campaigns and fiscal safeguards
Affordable housing, 13, 64
Agriculture, 24
Air quality, 12, 44
Alliance for Justice, 103, 189, 191–192
American Farmland Trust, 127, 188, 195, 197
American Red Cross, 18
American Statistical Association, 68, 188
American Viewpoint, 44, 64
Arnold, Missouri, 79
Asher, Thomas R., 103, 189, 191
Athens-Clarke County, Georgia, 156
Audit, independent. *See* fiscal safeguards
Audubon Society, 126
Austin, Texas, 58–59

Ballot measure, designing a winning
    ballot language, 21, 34, 36, 45, 49, 53-54, 76–77, 86, 88-92
    case study: Beaufort County measure reflects public tolerance
        for spending, 86
    case study: Colorado Community Approves Sales Tax Measure
        with Fiscal Safeguards, 92
    case study: Gallatin County, Montana, establishes the state's first
    purchase-of-development-rights program, 76
    checklist, 91

defining goals, identifying land, setting priorities, 75
determining acquisition methods, 75, 79
determining the best time, 81
establishing fiscal safeguards, 85. *See also* fiscal safeguards
fiscal safeguards checklist, 87
land trust partnerships, 80
naming properties, 78
qualifying an initiative, 90
selecting funding size and mechanism, 84
Barnes, Governor Roy, 95
Barton Creek, 58
Base voters, 51. *See also* campaigns
Beaufort County, South Carolina, 86, 180
Benefits of open space. *See* value of open space
Bernalillo County, New Mexico, 85
Better Jacksonville Plan, 4
Big Sur Land Trust, VII, 54
Bloomfield, Michael, 160
Boise, Idaho, VII, 49, 135, 166
Boise Foothills, VII, 49, 83, 135
Borrowing, 25–26, 31, 56, 84
Boulder, Colorado, 2, 88, 189, 191
Broadcast media. *See* campaigns
Broward County, Florida, 113–114
Brown, Corey, VII, 54, 90, 188
Brownfields, brownfield redevelopment, 4
Budget appropriation, 6, 15
Budgeting resources. *See* campaigns
Bush, Governor Jeb, 9
Business improvement districts, 30

Cable television, 96, 113, 129
Calendar, campaign, 121
California, 14–15, 68, 70, 89, 126, 130, 135
California Conservation Campaign, 130
California Park and Recreation Society, 127, 131
California State Parks Foundation, 131
Campaign manager. *See* campaigns
Campaigns
    advisory committees, 74, 76–78, 88, 92, 96, 106, 128, 134
    budgeting your resources, 122
    case study: Campaign Helps Launch Local Greenspaces Initiative
        (DeKalb County), 95
    designing a campaign plan and budget, 120
    designing an Internet campaign strategy, 166

designing a winning campaign strategy, 113

designing direct mail, 141. *See also* direct mail

developing a paid media plan, 138. *See also* paid media

headquarters and equipment, 112, 123

identifying base and swing voters, 116

keeping it legal, 94. *See also* legal

manager, 109–110, 135, 159, 173, 180

message and theme, 114

organizing your campaign, 106, 189

planning for free media 160. *See also* free media

posting house signs and billboards, 156

producing broadcast media, 152. *See also* paid media

raising money, 125. *See also* fundraising

running a conservation campaign, 93

securing endorsements, 136

setting up your field organization, 170. *See also* field

staff and volunteers, 104, 109, 112, 116

targeting analysis, 117, 171

timing your campaign activities, 121

working with campaign consultants, 157

Campaigns & Elections, 160, 189

Cape Cod, 185

Cape Cod, Massachusetts, 127

Case studies. *See* ballot measure. *See* fundraising. *See* campaigns

Cattleman's Association; 127

Charlotte, North Carolina; 5

Chevron/Texaco; 131

Clean Water, Safe Parks, and Community Trails
        Initiative (St. Louis), 42, 71, 136

Coastal Zone Management Program. *See* federal conservation funding sources

Coles, Mayor Brent (Boise, Idaho), 49, 81

Collins Tract, 79

Colorado, 2, 14–15, 55, 88, 92, 151, 186

Committee, citizens advisory. *See* fiscal safeguards and campaigns

Community assessment, 69

Community benefits. *See* value of open space

Community Preservation Act, 13, 64

Congestion Mitigation and Air Quality Improvement Program.
        See federal Conservation funding sources

Conservation Campaign, VII, IX, 80, 93, 100, 107, 123, 130, 169, 197

Conservation easements, 11, 76, 79, 86, 217

Conservation Finance Program, VII, IX, XI, 18, 197

Conservation finance, national trends in, 19

Conservation Foundation, 10, 44, 142

Conservation Fund, 10-12, 15, 80, 126, 194, 197

Conservation Spending Account. *See* federal conservation funding sources
Conservation tax credits, 14
Consultants. *See* campaigns
Cooperative Endangered Species Conservation Fund. *See* federal
    conservation funding sources
Costas, Bob, 136
County Open Lands and Trails Planning and Advisory
    Committee (COLTPAC), 88
Crime, 3, 52, 57, 60, 90
Cross-tabs, 48, 51, 54, 58-59

Dakota County, Minnesota, 107, 169
Danforth, Senator John C. (Missouri), 41, 136
Database, 124, 168, 182
DeKalb County, Georgia, 95, 126, 129, 167
Delaney, Mayor John (Jacksonville, Florida), 4
Delinquency, 3, 57, 75, 115
Democrats, 58, 141
Demographics. *See* research
Direct mail. *See* paid media
Disclaimers, 96, 99
Doak, Carrier, and O'Donnell, 70, 153, 188
Donatelli, Becky, 167, 189
Donor, 10, 104, 106, 111, 125–128, 130, 132, 134, 139, 167, 178
Drinking water, 3, 5, 24, 54, 57, 62, 64, 69, 70, 143, 179, 180
Ducks Unlimited, 126, 131, 197
DuPage County, Illinois, 57
Duvernoy, Eugene, VII

Economic benefits. *See* value of open space
Election analysis. *See* research
Election day, 15, 42, 51, 59, 96, 122, 139, 141, 146, 161, 170, 172, 175–176,
    179, 180–185
Election results, 37, 39
Endorsements, 38, 107, 140, 142, 149
Exempt purpose expenditures, 102–103

Farm Bureau, 127
Farmland, 1, 4, 11, 14, 16, 23, 42, 62, 75–77, 86, 92, 125, 144, 188, 195
Farmland Protection Program. *See* federal conservation funding sources
Feasibility assessment, 21, 76

    CONSERVATION FINANCE HANDBOOK

Federal conservation funding sources
    Coastal Zone Management Program, 11
    Congestion Mitigation and Air Quality Improvement Program, 12
    Conservation Spending Account, 6
    Cooperative Endangered Species Conservation Fund, 11
    Farmland Protection Program, 11
    Forest Legacy Program, 10
    Land and Water Conservation Fund, 10
    Migratory Bird Conservation Fund, 12
    National Coastal Wetlands Conservation, 12
    North American Wetlands Conservation Act, 11
    Transportation Efficiency Act for the 21st Century (TEA-21), 12
    Wetlands Reserve Program, 12
Feldman, Esther, VII, 36, 188
Field
    field coordinator, 111. *See also* campaign staff
    getting-out-the-vote, 173, 183
    nuts and bolts of tracking voters, 181
    organizing a speakers bureau, 180
    organizing neighborhood coffees and house parties, 178
    precinct captain, 172, 178, 181–182, 184
    sample phone scripts, 179
    setting up your field organization, 170
    volunteer phone banking, 174
    voting by mail (absentee ballot), 177
    walking door-to-door, 113, 172–173
Field coordinator. *See* campaign staff
Finance committee. *See* fundraising
Finance coordinator. *See* campaign staff
Financing options
    exploring federal, state, and private conservation funding sources, 6.
        See also local financing options. *See* also state conservation finance
        "best practices". *See* also federal conservation financing sources
Fiscal safeguards
    administrative costs, 86–87
    fiscal safeguards checklist, 87
    independent audit, 44, 50, 70, 76, 82, 86–87, 92, 153, 179
    Independent citizens committee, 87
    sunset clause, 17, 82, 86–87, 92
Foundations. *See* private conservation funding sources
Free media
    planning for free media, 160
    tips for talking with a reporter, 165
Funding quilt, 5–6

Fundraising
    case study: California Conservation Measures Attracts
        Widespread Support, 130
    case study: DeKalb County Campaign Beats the Clock, 129
    finance committee, III, 128–129, 132, 136
    fundraising techniques, 129
    raising money, 10, III, 125, 129, 132, 134, 157

Gallatin County, Montana, 21, 23, 75-76
Garden State Preservation Trust Act, 7
General obligation bond, 13, 26, 31-32, 44, 52, 56, 61, 76, 86, 95, 142
Georgia, 95, 118, 126, 156, 167
Get-out-the-vote. *See* field
Girl Scouts, 18
Glazer, Steven, VII, 16, 188
Glendening, Governor Parris, 7
Grants, 6–7, 9–10, 13
Grassroots lobbying, 102-103
Grazing, 24
Green Acres, 7, 13, 38
Green design, 1
Green infrastructure, 1, 7, 193–194
GreenPrint program (Maryland), 7
Greenprinting, understanding, 1
Grey, Judge Lawrence, 189, 191
Growth management, 2, 4, 7, 24, 187, 195
Gunnison County, Colorado, 2
Guzzetta, S. J., 94, 189

Hall Family Foundation, 8
Harrison, Ted, 58, 155
Health and environment benefits. *See* value of open space
Hilton Head Island, 86
Historic preservation, 12, 85, 197
House parties. *See* field

Illinois, IX, 41, 44, 57, 71, 88, 107, 138, 142
Impact fees, 30
Incentives, X, 3, 5–6, 13, 21, 78
Independent audits. *See* fiscal safeguards
Independents, 58
Infrastructure benefits. *See* value of open space
Initiative, 7, 15, 28, 34-35, 42, 62, 70, 90, 95, 102, 104
Internal Revenue Service (IRS), 96–97, 99, 100, 102, 104, 106
Internet. *See* campaigns
Inventory, 77

Jacksonville, Florida VII, 4, 188
Jones, Vernon (DeKalb County, Georgia), 95, 129
Joyner-Kersee, Jackie, 136

Kane County, Illinois, 44
Kansas City, Missouri, 8
Ketchum Public Relations, 165
Kitchens Group, 64

Land and Water Conservation Fund. *See* federal conservation funding sources
Land protection criteria
    development pressure, 78
    financial status, 78
    location, 77
    public support, 78
Land Trust Alliance, 18, 187, 192–193, 197, 217
Land trusts, XI, 1, 7, 9, 14, 18, 77, 80, 127, 130
Landuse, 3, 23–25, 38, 46
LandVote, 18, 187–188, 192
League of Conservation Voters, 126, 131
League of Women Voters, 59
Legal
    common legal mistakes, 106
    corporate campaign committees, 105
    federal, state, and local election laws, 96, 99
    Internal Revenue Service lobbying laws, 96, 102
    postal requirements, 96, 101
    researching legal contraints, 34
    state and local campaign finance laws, 96–97
Letters-to-the-editor, 117, 161–162, 164, 168
Loans, 13, 99
Lobbying, IX, 18, 97, 102–104, 106–107, 130
Local financing options
    common local financing options, 29
    local conservation funds: trends and techniques, 15
Los Angeles County, 35, 90, 188
Lotteries, 12

Maryland, 7, 14
Massachusetts, 13–14, 16, 64
Maui County, Hawaii, 108
McHenry County, Illinois, 142
Mecklenburg County, North Carolina, 151
Media. *See* campaigns

Media consultants. *See* campaigns
Mellman, Mark, 160, 188
Message. *See* campaigns
MetroGreen, 8. *See* also Kansas City, Missouri
Miami-Dade County, Florida, 52–53, 57, 75, 84, 87
Migratory Bird Conservation Fund. *See* federal conservation funding sources
Mining, 24
Missouri, 8, 41, 71, 79, 88, 107, 138
Montana, IX, 21, 75–76
Morris County, New Jersey, 107, 137
Mountain Island Lake, 5

Nash, Phil, 169, 189
Native Americans, 75, 131
New England, 15
New Jersey, 7, 13, 38, 56, 66, 137
New Mexico, 32, 73, 85
New West Policy Group, 155
New York, IX, 16, 189, 191–192
Newspaper. *See* free media
Newspaper advertising. *See* paid media
Nonprofit organization, IX, 6, 11, 13-14, 38, 87, 96, 101, 105, 107,
        125, 130, 149, 192

Ocean County, New Jersey, 38, 56, 66
Open Land and Trails Plan for the Wildlife Mountains, Trails,
        and Historic Places Program 74, 88
Opposition. *See* campaigns, identifying base and swing voters
Ormond Beach, Florida, 148

Packard Foundation, David and Lucille, 8
Paid media
        advertising in the newspaper, 149
        advertising on radio, 154
        advertising on television, 152
        designing direct mail, 141
        developing a plan, 138
        direct mail production, 145
        mechanics of bulk mail, 146
        posting house signs and billboards, 156
        radio scripts, 155
        television scripts, 153
        types of direct mail, 141
        working with consultants, 157

Partnerships, 9, 11, 14, 80
Pay-as-you-go, 25, 29
Peninsula Open Space Trust, 131
Pennsylvania, 14
Phone banks. *See* field
Pitkin County, Colorado, 151
Planning and Conservation League, 130
Playgrounds, 3, 16, 42, 179
Polling
    case studies (Boise, Idaho; Kane County, Illinois;
        Massachusetts), 44, 49, 64
    definition of polling terms, 51
    designing and interpreting your poll, 51
    interviewing community leaders, 43
    matrix, 60
    right poll and the right time, 50
    sample community survey questions, 45
    strongest supporters, 59
    studying results, 59
    threshold question, 51, 53, 176
    voters willing to spend, 22, 55
    what do voters want, 57
Pollster, selecting a, 46
Precinct captain. *See* field
Preservation Project, 4
Press secretary. *See* campaign staff
Private conservation funding sources, 4, 6
Property taxes, 7, 13, 25, 27, 29, 32, 38, 49, 62, 64, 76, 81, 85, 107–108,
    129, 185, 194
Proposition 12 (California), 69
Proposition 13 (California), 68
Proposition C (St. Louis), 42, 71, 88, 136, 138, 153
Public opinion. *See* polling
Purchase-of-development-rights, 14, 21, 76

Radio advertising. *See* paid media
Rating points, 152
Real estate transfer tax, 7, 13, 25, 29, 61, 127, 185
Recreational Trails Program. *See* federal conservation funding sources
Referendum, 15, 28, 34, 44, 79, 90, 114, 119, 142
Regulation, 3, 34, 89, 90, 97-98, 101, 106, 111, 147, 156
Reich, Brian, 168
Reporters, 111, 162, 164
Republicans, 38, 58, 117, 145

Research
    analyzing election data, 37
    basic demographics and landuse, 23
    common local financing options, 29
    conservation finance research case study, 32
    crunching the numbers, 26
    investigating financing options, 25
    local election analysis, 39
    research checklist: community profile, 24
    research checklist: election analysis, 38
    research checklist: financing options, 28
    research checklist: legal issues and constraints, 36
    researching legal constraints, 34
Revenue bonds, 13, 31, 33
Routt County, Colorado, 55–56

Safe Neighborhood Parks Act (Los Angeles), 35
Safe Neighborhood Parks Act (Miami-Dade County), 52, 84
Sales tax, sales and use tax, 4, 7, 12, 25–26, 33, 41, 56, 61, 71, 74, 79,
    84, 87–88, 92, 107, 119, 186
Sample (polling), 44, 46, 49, 59–60, 64, 66, 68, 87
Santa Fe County, New Mexico, 57, 73, 85, 88, 113, 155
Sierra Club, 126, 131
Skagit County, Washington, 8
Smart growth, 7–8, 193–194
Sortino, Peter, VII, 41, 72
South Carolina, 15, 86
Southampton, New York, 16
Speakers bureau. See field
Special assessment districts, 30
Spokespeople, 52, 116, 163, 185
St. Louis 2004, VII, 41, 71, 88
St. Louis, Missouri, 41–43, 71, 88, 136, 138, 153
Staff. See campaigns
State conservation finance "best practices"
    conservation tax credits, 14
    program of incentives for local governments, 13
    public-private partnerships, 11
    purchase-of-development-rights, 14, 21, 76
    significant local enabling options, 13
    substantial, dedicated state funding source, 12
State funding options. See state conservation finance "best practices"
Stearns Consulting, Inc., 43, 114
Strategy, designing a winning campaign, 113

Subset (polling), 47, 60, 145, 183
Sunset clause. *See* fiscal safeguards
Swing voters. *See* campaigns

Taxes, XI, 6, 12, 25, 38, 54, 58, 61, 64, 84, 92, 100, 129, 195
Television advertising. *See* campaigns
Ten ways to increase open space funds, 18
Theme. *See* campaigns
Top-lines (polling), 48, 51
Tourism, 18, 24, 29, 46, 62, 132, 193
Traffic, 22, 49–50, 61, 86, 115
Trails, 12, 41, 44, 58, 71, 76, 88, 155
Transportation, X, 3–4, 12
Transportation Efficiency Act. *See* federal conservation funding sources
Treasurer. *See* campaigns
The Trust for Public Land (TPL), VII, IX, 1, 12, 19, 21, 45, 79, 107, 122,
    126, 148, 151, 156, 187, 192, 196

U.S. Post Office, 96, 101, 146

Value of open space
    community benefits, 3
    economic benefits, 3
    fiscal benefits, 3
    flood prevention benefits, 3
    health and environmental benefits, 3
    infrastructure benefits, 3
Vermont, 14, 100
Virginia, 15
Volunteer coordinator. *See* campaigns
Volunteers. *See* campaigns
Voter counts, 145
Voter turnout, 35, 37, 39, 82, 91, 118, 145, 185
Voting-by-mail. *See* field

Walk program. *See* field
Washington, 8, 103, 118
Water quality, 4, 16, 22, 41, 44, 49, 57, 61, 68, 70, 76, 81, 86, 95,
    113, 125, 153, 193
Watershed, 4, 39, 44, 46, 59, 68, 85, 115, 130, 155, 179, 193
Web site, 96, 129, 146, 163, 166, 168, 169, 194
Wetlands Reserve Program. *See* federal conservation funding sources
Wildlife habitat, IX, 1, 41, 49, 57, 64, 79, 81, 185

Zoning, 3

To order other TPL publications, go to
WWW.TPL.ORG/PUBLICATIONS

LOCAL GREENPRINTING FOR GROWTH: Using Land
Conservation to Guide Growth and Preserve the Character
of our Communities
By Kim Hopper

This four-part series provides information and guidance to agencies
that protect open space. The reports focus on the the three steps of
Greenprinting, a long-term strategy for guiding development and
growth. The first volume is an overview and introduction. The final
three volumes describe the Greenprinting process:

· Defining a Conservation Vision
· Securing Conservation Funds
· Acquiring and Managing Park and Conservation Lands

$15 FOR EACH. $25 FOR ALL FOUR VOLUMES.

THE EXCELLENT CITY PARK SYSTEM: What Makes it Great
and How to Get There
By Peter Harnik

In 1997, TPL began collecting and publishing data on the nation's
park systems. TPL initially focused on park funding and acreage in
the nation's largest cities. This new 48-page publication expands
data collection to 55 cities and offers a new seven-point framework
for determining park excellence. This breakthrough report also
details examples of exceptional practices. "Understanding the value
of city parks begins with knowing what factors can make our city
parks great."

$15

CONSERVATION EASEMENT HANDBOOK
Co-published with the Land Trust Alliance
By Elizabeth Byers and Karin Marchetti Ponte

Conservation easements are the premier legal tool for addressing
private land conservation priorities in America's communities.
This handbook—a completely revised and expanded update of the
1988 original—is the definitive practical and technical resource on
conservation easements and best practices for their use. The use
of conservation easements has evolved to address a wide array of
landscapes, and this handbook will assist conservation professionals
with navigating the legal complexities of their protection efforts.

$40

PROTECTING THE SOURCE: Land Conservation and the Future of America's Drinking Water
By Caryn Ernst

This report is part of an on-going effort by TPL and the American
Water Works Association to promote land conservation as part of
a multiple barrier approach to drinking water protection. Protecting
the Source explores scientific, economic, and public health rationales
for using land conservation for drinking water protection and
presents best practices for successful implementation locally.

$15

LANDVOTE 2003: Americans Invest in Parks and Open Space
By Matt Zieper

Overwhelming support from American voters for local and state land
conservation funding continues in 2003, as documented by
this new report. *LandVote 2003* is a review of the ballot measures
in 2003 that brought over $2 billion in land conservation-related
dollars to over 100 communities across America. This informative
report also includes success stories about local conservation
finance measures.

FREE